THROUGH DESERT PLACES

A Version of Psalms 1–50

JIM COTTER

SHEFFIELD
CAIRNS PUBLICATIONS
1989

CONTENTS

iv   *Contents*

PREFACE

This version of the first fifty psalms of the Hebrew Psalter is neither translation nor paraphrase. Nor does it pretend to be anything more felicitous than passable rhythmic prose. But it does draw on the original for inspiration and theme, and sometimes for specific words and phrases. The aim has been to make the Psalms prayable for those who find stumbling blocks in many of them as they have been variously translated into English. The reasoning behind this process of adaptation is explained in the Introduction.

The psalms in this version have been laid out on the page so that they can be used either by the individual praying alone or by groups praying together. One voice, or a few, could say or even chant the sections, with the whole company responding with the refrain at the end of each section. There could be a period of silence at the end of those sections, before the prayer which reflects the theme of the psalm.

Why it is that groups of people tend to shout when reading the Psalms together – especially clergy – is a puzzle. Certainly the mood of some of these verses is exultant, and then a shout is appropriate. But surely in use it is best to be sensitive to the various moods, and on the whole to speak slowly and quietly. I suspect that the unthinking bellow owes much to the way in which many of the Psalms have become routine and remote.

I owe a debt of gratitude to Alan Ecclestone for his foreword. His book *Yes to God* argues powerfully for prayer to be connected with the details of our everyday life, both individual and corporate. The version of the Psalms in these pages has been written with the need for that connection very much in mind.

Jim Cotter
Sheffield, July 1989

FOREWORD

How to remedy the spiritual impoverishment of our time among the peoples of the so-called First World culture? To an increased extent we have become aware in the realms of physical and mental well-being of the parts played by diet, exercise, and environment. Of spiritual health, the health of persons and communities in their lives and relationships, we have been and still are recklessly careless. We can ill-afford to continue to be spendthrift in this most vital and fundamental area of our human condition.

To what resources and directives shall we turn? What spiritual exercises could we profitably undertake to recover some greater measure of wholeness and health? We recall what men like St Benedict and St Ignatius did for their generations, what Law and Boehme did for theirs. We have seen among our contemporaries what remarkable help has been gained from renewed acquaintance with Julian of Norwich and works like *The Cloud of Unknowing*. More rich in sustenance, more tested by experience, more illuminative in perception, nevertheless, are the Psalms of David. For Jews and Christians alike, they have for centuries been the main channel of spiritual nourishment to innumerable men and women. To an extent we can scarcely begin to assess their words have passed into the fabric of religious life and thought.

We need to be more aware of their significance for our present needs. The Psalms are not monuments to be piously acknowledged by passers-by. They are words to be absorbed, insights to be observed, songs to be sung, commitments to be made our own. It is now almost five centuries since Erasmus wrote of the translation of the Scriptures then being made available: ''I long that the husbandman should sing portions of them to himself as he follows the plough, that the weaver should hum them to the tune of his shuttle, that the traveller should beguile with their stories the tedium of his journey.'' Ploughing, weaving, travelling have changed greatly, but we stand no less in need of the songs of Zion today.

That they should be made available, attractive, and relevant to our generation is the aim and purpose of their presentation in this book, in the re-working of translations, and in the added reflections

vii

and suggested usage. Inevitably those of us who have long memories of the psalmody of the Book of Common Prayer will be conscious of the displacement of cherished phrases. Many may query the appropriateness of some of the revisions. Others will wonder whether the old bottles can really serve to convey the new wine that is being presented through them. Only practice can prove the worth of the new forms provided.

That worth will be tested and attested in a number of ways. The new turns of phrase should open to us new insights into the Psalmist's rich and enduring spirituality. The extended phraseology can help to intertwine the reflections of the Psalmist evoked by his circumstances with those which are born of our present day issues. That we are in the midst of a language crisis is a commonplace observation today. The problems of translation will not go away but rather increase year by year. What is attempted in this presentation of the Psalms is a supremely important and necessary task for which we have good reason to be grateful. It deserves to be used painstakingly and attentively in our own pilgrim's progress.

No other body of literature has ever so knit together the yearnings, hopes, sufferings, joy, and intentions of persons and people in their day to day life and their life before God as the Psalms. That relationship, personal and corporate, is our spiritual lifeline. This version, done in today's English, is designed to help in the rejuvenation of the perception of our calling as God's children, servants, friends, and fellow-workers.

Alan Ecclestone
Gosforth, June 1989

INTRODUCTION

It is hard for us to imagine what it was like for the human beings who discovered fire. For the first time they could feel relatively safe and warm at night. Not for nothing do we still talk of hearth and home. Round a fire intimacies are shared, stories are told, ballads are sung. Tell us what God is like. Tell us about our ancestors. Sing us one of the songs of our people.

In some such fertile soil we may guess the seeds of the Psalms were sown, with their all too human experiences of grief, indignation, gratitude, and awe, some of them intimate and tender, others more formally telling a story suitable for acclamation and celebration in a holy place on a holy day. In the Psalms we read soul-deep into the life of a people and the life of individuals. Indeed, their minds and hearts swung so easily between identifying with the one and then with the many that they could pray as 'I' or as 'We' with equal facility, changing the one to the other without any sense of mismatch in meaning and intention.

We glimpse, too, their beliefs, and the way they were inspired to put into words their individual and corporate experience of God. At their best, those words are shaped into a poetry where the meaning of that experience is heightened, where it is made memorable, re-callable, renewable.

Some of the Psalms may indeed have been composed white-hot by a now unknown man or woman. But they would not have survived in common prayer if either the experience or the poetry had been quirky and inaccessible to others. This is one of the extraordinary features of some of these poems (some are indifferent verse), that human beings of other cultures and in other historical periods have recognized themselves in these words, from their self-pity and self-righteousness through their honest laments, complaints, and anger, to their quiet contentment and exuberant joy. Not only that – they have been able to pray with, in, and through those words.

Yet there are questions too. Some of the Psalms lack self-criticism. There is no clue that self-righteousness (even if clothed in seeming God-righteousness) should provoke repentance. There is no questioning of brutal feelings and cruel deeds. (If God is

angry, you can plunder at will.) The contexts of many of the details
of the people's story have been lost, so that they are no longer the
bearers of meaning. Some of the metaphors, pastoral and military
and patriarchal, are now distant from most of us.

But we do not need to use all of the Psalms just as they are. Too
easily do we seem to fall prey to the fundamentalism of 'what is
given must be used entire.' It may be convenient to have material
for prayer bound in one book, but this does not necessarily mean
that everything in that book must be used. Convenience should not
be interpreted as compulsion. If we believe in the Spirit of God
guiding us into the truth and creating all things new, then some of
us will feel bound to respond to the invitation actually to participate
in the process of shaping words of prayer. Over a period of time we
should expect to be making alterations in the margin and putting
question marks.

Christians need to be more robust. Surely we can, like our less
inhibited Jewish brothers and sistes, continue to argue with God
and with our ancestors. We can use metaphors that directly
connect, without a dislocation of our imagination, for those of us
praying in English in today's world. We can illuminate or contrast
the Hebrew Psalms by reference to the New Testament and to
Christian writings since, as well as with boldness and humility
bring to bear our more contemporary insights into the workings
of human relationships and communities.

Here are some examples from this book:

> The voice of my heart has impelled me:
> Seek the face of the living God.
> Out of the darkness I discern your presence
> in the face of the Risen Christ,
> revealing your pain and your joy,
> in new and abundant life. [27]

The original Psalm 15 describes the characteristics of those who are
just in their ways. In this version there is an added section:

> Those who recognize the outcast as the one whom they need,
> who forgive to seventy times seven,
> who depend on the mercy of God,
> and live the highest law that is Love. [15]

The version of the 'royal' psalm, 45, includes reference to the kingship of Jesus:

> We praise you, O God,
> for the gift of yourself in the Infant King:
> Jesus, sovereign ruler of all,
> in whom is our royal destiny too. [45]

The suggested refrains for Psalms 4 and 11 echo Julian of Norwich:

> All manner of thing shall be well. [4]

> As a hazelnut lies in the palm of my hand,
> so I rest secure in the presence of God. [11]

Psalm 9b has been inspired by Alan Ecclestone's book *The Night Sky of the Lord* (Darton, Longman, & Todd, 1980), probing as it does the mysterious ways of God in a century of holocaust:

> We stare dumbly at the death camps of hell:
> Lo! Dark evil is crowned
> in the midst of the tortured and dying.
> The needy are forgotten,
> the oppressed know not the stronghold of God. [9b]

And the version of Psalm 5 begins by incorporating an approach to prayer at the beginning of the prayer itself:

> At the turning of the day
> I make ready for my prayer,
> emptying my mind, opening my heart,
> my whole self watching and waiting. [5]

In conversation about this book, Alan Ecclestone pondered the question as to why there has never been a collection of Christian Psalms. I wonder if this reflects the different histories of the Jewish and Christian peoples. The Hebrew Psalter expresses the faith of a small people in a small land, never feeling secure, often internally at odds, with a nomadic streak to the corporate temperament, and with the experience of exile deeply seared into them. Christianity has always been more dispersed, almost from the beginning, has never been the religion of only one nation, and has never had as part of its Scriptures writings of a date later than a hundred years from those beginnings.

We sometimes forget that the New Testament powerfully opens up Christian faith but that it reflects only the experience of the first few generations, not that of hundreds of years. Unfortunately, the Church has often sealed off, as it were, that faith by formally declaring what was inspired and containing it within a book. So it has been outside the Scriptures that the Christian form of 'psalms' has developed, ie the vast collection of hymns. And these have been written in different languages in different centuries, for different occasions. They have been added to, altered, forgotten, and rediscovered. This book ventures to continue that process, but in relation to the Psalms themselves, in the hope that, as with the adaptations, omissions, and additions to medieval hymns, they can be made more directly prayable in our own day.

Certainly at the end of this millenium, there is a pressure upon us to outgrow our earlier loyalties to a particular country and to a particular interpretation of a religious inheritance. We are being pressed protestingly into the experience of becoming citizens of one world. Each religion is being challenged to look again at its tendencies to be exclusive and hostile to others. There is the possibility of a new connecting of the particularities of metaphors and the universalities of human experience in a predominantly urban culture – issues nuclear and ecological on a vulnerable planet, with T-shirts and jeans, cars and bicycles, traffic lights and television, airports and offices, propaganda and terrorism, viruses and bacteria in bloodstream and food, in every city of the world.

So, in these versions of the Psalms –

> . . . invisible rain falls on the mountains,
> even the caves fill with rubble. [11]

> Save us from the corruption of language,
> from manipulators of words, greedy for power. [12]

> In country lanes we have hidden and pounced,
> in city streets we have stalked and murdered. [10]

> The young prowl the streets and precincts,
> alienated, rootless, pain turning to violence. [9]

In the Hebrew Psalm 22, which Jesus may have prayed as he was dying, there is the picture of the huntsmen and their dogs encircling the victim. In this version similar experiences are added from our own century: the prisoner in the concentration camp, the patient in hospital gasping for air, the person quarantined and left alone by those who withdraw in terror.

Again, widening the vision, the laws of God

> ...dance as the stars of the universe,
> perfect as the parabolas of comets,
> like satellites and planets in their orbits,
> reliable and constant in their courses. [19]

We are called to be stewards of the planet:

> How awesome a task
> you entrust to our hands;
> how fragile and beautiful
> is the good earth. [8]

When that good earth was more forested than it is now, only sporadically settled, it is not surprising that those over the mountains or across the river, unknown and possibly more powerful, were feared as enemies. Nor is it surprising that wars broke out over disputed territory as the population grew and the land was cleared. Only in our generation have we reached the point where co-operation for the sake of the survival of the planet is rendering war a wasteful, outmoded, and increasingly suicidal means of resolving conflict.

As our consciousness changes, the use of many of the Psalms becomes more and more problematic. They assume a stance of 'over-againstness', of enemies beyond the gates, and of claims for God on our side. 'We' are innocent in our integrity while 'they' are spurned as hypocrites and deceivers. To our ears this sounds shrill and defensive. We have suffered – and still do suffer – from so-called 'holy' wars.

By contrast, and very slowly over the centuries, we have seen glimpses of a different understanding of God, who indeed strives with those who rebel against the ways and laws of Love, but who seeks always to redeem tragedy and to travel the second mile in pursuit of those who are bewildered and lost. The problem arises from our persistent refusal to recognize this truth. We continue to project on to God our suspicion of the stranger, so that we can self-righteously slaughter our enemies on God's behalf.

You can see these two viewpoints struggling with each other in different people's attitudes to the words of Jesus (reported in John 8) to the woman who had been caught in the act of adultery. Having challenged her accusers to throw the first stone only if they were themselves without sin, he says to the woman, "Neither do I condemn you; go, and do not sin again." (John 8.ii) Some people emphasize the first part of that sentence, others the second. But what do you think Jesus would have said to the person who asked him, "What if she commits adultery again?" If you focus on "Go, and do not sin again," you might well venture to say, "Well, she was given a second chance, but now the law must take effect and she must be stoned." If you focus on "Neither do I condemn you," you might say, "I cannot condemn you, though you are brought to me seventy times seven." But the sorrow in the voice and the hurt in the eyes might make the questioner pause. Here is one who bears the pain of her and my and our sin, one who feels it right through. And this might evoke the response, "Let me share the pain too. Let me stop acting in ways that hurt you. You are so utterly loving, so totally attractive, that I cannot but love you in return." I think that is the way of the Gospel, recognized in moments of reconciliation and joy.

If we seek to transform our praying of the Psalms in this light, then we must pray our way, with clarity and hope, *through* this process of recognition and reconciliation. Certain stages can be discerned:

1   Honestly admitting our hostile feelings:

> Slay them with your iron fist,
> may they choke on the grapes of your wrath, [17]

2   Becoming aware of our own hatreds and potential for evil:

> Purge me of hatred and smugness,
> of self-righteous satisfied smile. [17]

This is a discipline of becoming less judgmental of others and more sternly truthful with ourselves:

> Forgive the boast of your people, O God,
> self-righteous and blind in our mouthings. [26]

3 Becoming aware too of the forces that threaten us from within as well as from others:

> I am afraid of the powers that prowl within me,
> howling in the dark of the moonless nights. [3]

4 Recognizing the Love that is expressed through both judgment and mercy:

> You thunder so fiercely in love for us,
> you whisper so gently in judgment. [50]

5 Focusing this awareness in contemplation of Christ, recognizing that the extremes of some of our prayer need to be tempered:

> Do not be mocked or derided, O God:
> speak to us in your wrath,
> terrify us in your fury. . .

> But who *is* this, God's Chosen One, God's *Son*?
> Inheritor of the earth and all its people?
> You take our rage upon yourself,
> mocked and crucified, yet meeting all with love. [2]

6 Being brought to true repentance, through a clear recognition of ourselves in relation to God:

> Ah, Fire that shrivels up our hates,
> and brings us to our knees in awe!
> Ah, Light that pierces all our fury,
> laying bare our greed and pride!
> Forgive us, for we know not what we do. [2]

God's Love is stern but not vindictive. In the imagery of fire, it refines but does not utterly destroy. God brings good out of seeming total evil, a good that is beyond our imagining, yet the hope of which can become embedded in our prayer.

7 Offering ourselves, willing a new direction:

> Dear God, we offer you our lives this day,
> the gift of love in our hearts and our loins,
> the incense of prayer, the myrrh of our suffering,

the gold of all that we hold most dear. . . [45]

The kindness of course extends to our own enemy within:

Blessed are those who care for the poor and the helpless,
who are kind to the outcast within them. [41]

In some such way I believe it is possible for us to draw closer to
the true and living God, overcoming the unnecessary distancing
that we experience when trying to pray some of the Psalms in their
original form.

There is another such effect in those Psalms which retell the
details of the stories of the ways in which God has acted in the lives
of the people. Inevitably they do not bring God alive for us in the
same way as those who were but a generation or two from the
events. Only if we can imaginatively leap the centuries can we
make them part of our own story. Moreover, the history is written
in the third person, which makes it difficult to pray this kind of
psalm directly.

Two changes can help us here. One is to alter the grammar so
that the words become a more direct prayer to God in I-You
language: immediately the psalm becomes more engaging and
involving. (Such dialogue at least keeps us open to the possibility
of a relationship with a presence that we may for the time being
experience as absence: the rumour of God is still kept alive.)

The other is to refer to the present and the future as well as to the
past, petition and hope becoming part of the prayer as well as
thanksgiving or penitence. We need to take seriously the Hebrew
sense of the continuing activity of God: creation is not so much a
matter of a past event as of a ceaseless active process. Psalm 33 in
this version gives a perspective on the history and on creation,
Psalm 48 expands on the theme of Jerusalem as the City of God.

These variants and changes are not without risk, for they may
betray truth. We must keep on prising open our own twentieth
century assumptions that they may be tested by past wisdom, just
as we must have the courage to say that our ancestors were
sometimes wrong. (The Church, like the individuals in it, has
never been very good at admitting error.) So the task of renewal
and re-shaping needs to be attempted in a spirit of humility, yet
hoping, perhaps fancifully, that those same ancestors may one day

be eager to learn what new things God has revealed to us through our questing spirit in our own generation. It may even be that truth will dawn on us in the midst of the very process of arguing with those half-forgotten and shadowy people of faith. But the mood must be humble and not querulous, in a constant interaction between them and ourselves in prayer to and in God.

Now these versions cannot match the poetry of the English translations of the sixteenth century. For example, I am glad my mind has stored the sixth verse of Psalm 84 in the Book of Common Prayer:

> Who going through the vale of misery use it for a well,
> and the pools are filled with water.

Those words haunt me both in style and content. I cannot but appreciate having been exposed as a boy to the Elizabethan English of the Book of Common Prayer, Shakespeare, and the King James Bible. No English written today, whether American, British, International Standard, or one of the many global dialects, can pretend to be a substitute for it. At its best it is indeed glorious and memorable. As poetry and drama there is much that is still accessible: there are indeed gems to be treasured.

But there is much that is linguistically archaic and theologically questionable. There are those who will *claim* that the Book of Common Prayer is incomparable, the implication seeming to be that it is uniformly wonderful. But such theoretical fundamentalisms tend to be selective in practice. The well-thumbed Prayer Book and Bible is well-thumbed only in parts. I doubt there is a Shakespeare fan who has seen *Henry VI* as often as *King Lear*. Very few people have studied and absorbed the whole of Shakespeare or of the Bible or of the Book of Common Prayer: our knowledge of *Timon of Athens*, *Obadiah*, and *A Commination* is scanty. Most worshippers and theatre-goers come away from church or theatre generally impressed and possibly moved, but with few lines ringing in their heads. Maybe this simply shows how philistine are the British. I wonder. Even the 'treasury' of the Psalter in practice means two or three dozen Psalms, plus a few memorable fragments from elsewhere.

So a modest effort, not to replace, but to place alongside, may be helpful as an encouragement to pray. The versions of the Psalms in these pages may prove to be too banal and prosaic for continued use. We may wish to be selective, returning to the Elizabethan translations from time to time, even learning Hebrew in order to pray in the original. But the experience of praying the Psalms in a more contemporary way may release something of their spiritual power and enable us to 'taste and see' the gracious God afresh. I can only pray that the words do not indeed betray that graciousness. The warning in the version here of Psalm 5 must be heard by us, in whatever language we are attempting to pray:

> Our speeches are honeyed with peace,
> smooth words slide from our lips.
> The wavelengths dance with lies,
> siren songs deceptive in the dark. [5]

Yes, I am haunted by those words from Psalm 84, quoted above – and I am so haunted in a deeper sense. They are beautiful, but their truth is tough as well as glistening. They challenge us to dig deep into faith's uncompromising terrain and they encourage us with the hope that water will spring up in desert places. That can sustain us awhile. But when the drill that is biting into the rock breaks yet again, and the heat of the day echoes the harsh landscape, what then? In such unpromising circumstances, many of the Psalms were created, in an anguished faith in an absent God. It is because of this above all that they have resonated soul-deep in human beings ever since. In our day, at least in the First World, they resonate with the cries of a whole culture awry.

If there is a God, only a pain-bearing God can help. That is the hope, and that keeps us to the possibility of praise.

> Many are the afflictions of those who seek good,
> but the pain-bearing God is with them.
> You penetrate to the heart of their suffering,
> that they come to no lasting harm. [34]

And in the words of the prayer that follows that psalm:

> *Pain-bearer God, in our affliction we sense your presence,*
> *moving with our sufferings to redeem them, bringing joy*
> *out of tragedy, creating such music as the world has not*
> *yet heard. We praise you with great praise.*

If such faith holds, it does so only just. And it does so in the very act of falling into an abyss. We do not know whether we shall crash on the rocks, nor how fearful it will be to fall into the hands of the living God. Will it be that underneath are the everlasting arms, or will the great white bird of the southern seas that is the Spirit of God seize us and teach us how to fly?

PSALMS 1-50

PSALMS 1-50

THE TWO WAYS – A WISDOM SONG

Refrain: Keep us true to your Way.

Woe to us when we walk in the way of wickedness,
when we bend our ear to the counsel of deceit,
and scoff at what is holy from the seat of pride.

Blessings upon us when we delight in the truth of God,
and ponder God's Law by day and by night,
when we stand up for truth in face of the lie,
when we mouth no slogans and betray no friends.

Then we shall grow like trees planted by streams of water,
that yield their fruit in due season,
whose leaves do not wither.

We struggle with evil in our hearts,
tossed to and fro like chaff in the wind,
a rootless people whose lives have no meaning,
unable to stand when judgment comes,
desolate, outside the house of our God.

May ways of wickedness perish among us:
forgive us, O God, and renew us,
lead us in paths of justice and truth,
obedient to your Wisdom and Will,
trusting in the hope of your promise.

Giver of life, save us from the desert of faithlessness and nourish us with the living water of your Word, that we may bring forth fruit that will last, in the name of Jesus Christ our Saviour.

GOD'S ANOINTED ONE

Refrain: Come, refining fire of Love.

WHY do the nations rage at one another?
Why do we plot and conspire?
The powerful of the earth set themselves high,
the people collude with their pride.
We whisper against those God anoints,
chosen to embody God's will.

Do not be mocked and derided, O God:
speak to us in your wrath, terrify us in your fury,
break us with your rod of iron, bring us in fear and trembling
to fall down before you and kiss your feet.

But who *is* this, God's chosen one – God's *Son*?
Inheritor of the earth and all its people?
You take our rage upon yourself,
mocked and crucified, yet meeting all with love.

Ah, Fire that shrivels up our hates,
and brings us to our knees in awe!
Ah, Light that pierces all our fury,
laying bare our greed and pride!
Forgive us, for we know not what we do.

Come, wondrous Ruler of the universe,
holy and just, compassionate and merciful.
Come, universal Reign of peace.
Come, Anointed One, in glory!

*Ruler of heaven and earth, raising Jesus from the dead and giving him the victory,
work in us the power of your saving love and bring us to share in your reign;
through Jesus Christ our Saviour.*

THE STRUGGLE BETWEEN FEAR AND TRUST

Refrain: Your steadfast love never fails.

O GOD, how many are my foes.
They rise up against me,
surrounding me in the night,
adversaries and friends alike,
whispering that you cannot help me.

But you are a shield about me,
you are my glory, and you lift my head high.
I cry to you as I sleep and as I wake,
and the voice of your Presence sustains me.

I am afraid of the powers that prowl within me,
howling in the dark of the moonless night.
I tremble at the thousands and thousands
of weapons and armies swarming around me.
Arise, O God, deliver me: smite them on the cheek,
break their teeth, grind them to the dust.

No, do not destroy them: call out to them,
Rebellious powers, lay down your arms,
return to the God who made you.
Cease your oppression and fury,
and seek the mercies of God.

Liberator, setting us free,
your blessing be upon your people.

*Shield and protector of all, hear the prayers of those who call upon you, and set
them free from violence, persecution, and fear, that all may know the deliverance
that belongs to you alone. We ask this in the name of Jesus our Liberator.*

THE PEACE OF GOD

Refrain: *All manner of thing shall be well.*

ANSWER me when I call, O God
for you are the God of Justice.
You set me free when I was hard-pressed:
be gracious to me now and hear my prayer.

Men and women,
how long will you turn my glory to my shame?
How long will you love what is worthless
and run after lies?

Know that God has shown me such wonderful kindness.
When I call out in prayer, God hears me.

Tremble, admit defeat, and sin no more.
Look deep into your heart before you sleep, and be still.

Bring your gifts, just as you are,
and put your trust in God.

Many are asking, Who can make us content?
The light of your countenance has gone from us, O God.

Yet you have given my heart more gladness
than those whose corn and wine and oil increase.
I lie down in peace and sleep comes at once,
for in you alone, O God, do I dwell unafraid.

Faithful defender, do not let our hearts be troubled, but fill us with such confidence and joy that we may sleep in peace and rise in your presence; through Jesus Christ our Saviour.

A PRAYER FOR REPENTANCE

Refrain: Gently turn my face to the sun.

At the turning of the day
I make ready for my prayer,
emptying my mind, opening my heart,
my whole self watching and waiting.

Out of the silence comes my cry,
the groaning of my spirit,
profound, beyond words.
O God my Deliverer, listen, and answer.

You take no delight in wickedness:
evil may not sojourn with you.
The boastful may not stand before your eyes,
the proud wither at your glance.
You silence those who speak lies,
you withstand the thrust of the vengeful.

Only through the gift of your steadfast love
do I dare to enter your presence.
I will worship in your holy house
in fear and in trembling.
So easy is it to fall in false ways –
lead me, O God, in your justice,
make my path straight before me.

For there is no truth in our mouths,
our hearts are set on destruction,
our throats are an open sepulchre,
we flatter with our tongue.

Our speeches are honeyed with peace,
smooth words slide from our lips.
The wavelengths dance with lies,
siren songs deceptive in the dark.

Refrain: *Gently turn my face to the sun.*

Make us feel together the weight of our guilt,
let us fall by the burden of our deceits,
crumbling by reason of our trespass,
lost because of our rebellion.

Pluck us from the despair that follows the lie,
no longer weighed down with the burden of falsehood.
Strengthen our steps in obedience to truth,
turn our lamentation to dancing and joy.
Set us on fire with unquenchable love:
we shall honour your name, exulting with praise.

Blessed be God,
showering blessings on the just and the unjust.
Blessed be God,
enduring with us the showers of black rain.
Blessed be God,
shuddering with pain when sirens wail.
Blessed be God,
our blasts but a feather in the wind of the Spirit.
Blessed be God,
our evil but a drop in the ocean of love.
Blessed be God,
redeeming our wastes and our sorrows.
Blessed be God.

Source of all justice and goodness, hating deception and evil, lead us in the paths
of truth and godliness, and keep us from all lasting harm. So shall we sing out
our joy in you, O Christ the Living Truth, our Redeemer.

A DESPERATE CRY IN TIME OF ILLNESS

Refrain: *I cry out to the Void:*
                 How long, O God, how long?

HIDEOUS afflictions of a turbulent age –
virus, cancer, thrombosis, ulcer –
warheads in the fluids of my being:
I am caught in a world that is twisted,
trapped in its web of corruption,
tempted to blame my ills on to 'them',
tempted to avoid the hatred within.

Hard pressed by anxiety and discord,
carriers of disease, injectors of poison,
overwhelmed by malice and fear.
Paralysed, depressed, we cannot move,
spun in the vortex of death.

Distressed in the very depths of our being,
bones shaking, cells mutating,
we are almost in despair.

In your mercy and grace set us free.
Refine us in the fire of your love.
Our cry is of hope, yet struggling with doubt,
a stammer gasping for breath in the night.

Turn your face to me, save my life;
deliver me in the endurance of love,
ease the burden of guilt and of pain,
let me know the grace of your presence,
now in this life and through the shades of the grave.

I am weary with my suffering,
every night I flood my bed with tears.
I drench my couch with weeping,
my eyes waste away out of grief,
I grow weak through the weight of oppression.

Refrain: *I cry out to the Void:*
                   How long, O God, how long?

You that work evil and seek to destroy,
loosen your grip, away from my presence.
For God has heard the sound of my weeping,
forgives me with delight and lightens my gloom.
The destroyers will be ashamed and sore troubled:
trembling, they will be stripped of their power,
no longer able to harm.

And no, I will not gloat or hate,
in the Love of God I will hold on to you yet.
In the anger and hope of the wrath of our God,
come to the place of repentance and mercy.
And you, silent virus, invisible, malignant,
bound up with my bodily being,
are you an enemy that I can befriend,
or at least contain in a place of your own –
your power to harm taken away,
brought with us to the glory of God?

God of mercy and tenderness, giver of life and conqueror of death, look upon our
weakness and pain, and bring us to health and to wholeness, that we may sing
a new song to your praise; through Jesus Christ, Redeemer of the powers.

A SOCIETY IN FRAGMENTS

Refrain: Judge of the world, come and save us.

O GOD, we are shaken by terror,
our hearts grow cold through fear.
The lions roar, their teeth are bared,
they pounce at our throats and tear us apart.

The powers that be stand over us,
whispering treason to workers for peace,
declaring redundant the awkward and angular,
destroying by rumour the worth of a name.

Old loyalties no longer bind us,
family, neighbourhood, union, factory.
The young prowl the streets and the precincts,
alienated, rootless, pain turning to violence.
And the old, the weak, and the poor all cringe,
their welfare, their lives, threatened and vulnerable.

Your will for us, dear God, is sure and steady,
that we do justly, love mercy,
and walk humbly in your Way.
You would not have us return evil for evil,
plundering our enemies and requiting our friends.

Who can stand in your presence
with righteousness and integrity of heart?
Our hearts and our minds conceive evil:
they are pregnant with mischief and bring forth lies.
We dig the pit of our doom,
and fall into the hole we have made.

Our wickedness returns on our head,
we are crushed by the violence we have spawned.
Our lives are trampled to the ground,
our very being spent in the dust.

Refrain: Judge of the world, come and save us.

We cannot but sense your love as your wrath,
Judge of the world come with dread to save us.
Who can stand against the blast of your fury,
fiery shafts sprung from your bow?
Who can bear the anguish and pain in your eyes
as you scour and cleanse us with lasers?

And yet we give you thanks and praise,
for you will not let us go into the Void.
You bear the cost of our redeeming,
the Judge of all the world does right,
bringing us through tears to love for our neighbour,
leading us in pathways to glory and peace.

Judge and Saviour, pierce the secrets of our hearts and bring to light our hidden sins. Purify and strengthen us in faith, and give us courage to strive with evil and bear witness to your just and loving realm. This we pray according to the Way and in the Name of Jesus Christ our Redeemer.

STEWARDS OF CREATION

Refrain: *Creator God, Source of all life,*
            how gloriously does your name resound,
            echoing to the bounds of the universe!

THE morning stars sing for joy, and the youngest child cries
      your name.
The weak in the world shame the strong, and silence the
      proud and the rebellious.

When I look at the heavens, even the work of your fingers,
the moon and the stars majestic in their courses –
the eagle riding the air, the dolphin ploughing the sea,
the gazelle leaping the wind, the sheep grazing the fells –
who are we human beings that you keep us in mind,
children, women, and men that you care so much for us?

Yet still you bring us to life, creating us after your image,
stewards of the planet you give as our home.
How awesome a task you entrust to our hands.
How fragile and beautiful is the good earth.

Creator God, amid the immensities of the universe you seek us out and call us to
be partners in your work of creating. May we not fail you.

A PRAYER FOR CONCILIATORS

Refrain: *O God, steady our nerve that we may see clearly:*
          strengthen our will in working for peace.

NUCLEAR within and without, we are breaking apart:
cells disintegrating; virus and cancer;
the splitting of atoms; a new black death;
terrorists' dens burrowing the suburbs.

The tired game goes on, the reeds of the world trembling:
pre-emptive strikes; the tactics of bullies;
inaccurate bombings; one cell is blasted.

Hydra-like the desperate multiply:
the smallest of bombs lost in a suitcase:
revenge in mind, no matter who suffers.

Tares and wheat − can you tell them apart?
Neighbour subversive, our own heart corrupt.

International law − not my country right or wrong,
muscle frightened of wasting sickness.
Rational policing − not the sheriff's bully.
Restraining force at a minimum −
not the unleashing of eagle or bear.
Sanctions hurting us − no wonder we're reluctant.
Complexity recognized − simple solutions are final.

Can the powerful admit they have limits?
Give up their arrogance?
Know their own despair?
Understand desperate folk?

Work on in hidden ways, brave conciliators in conflicts:
patriots of earth: allied to no state, not even their own;
loyal to a future not one of us sees;
immaculately suited aliens in the strangest of lands.

Those locked in conflict − do they not see?
they all want their grandchildren
to breathe the good air.

Courage, bomb disposers who delve hearts and minds:
ease the finger from the trigger and button;
defuse the boiling fury, open the eyes blinded with rage.

You will come away wounded, paying a price for us all.
But judgment and mercy: these alone are left now.
We must love one another − or die.

O God of Wisdom, as we pray for those who are burdened with the tasks of negotiation among the peoples of the world, steady our nerves and strengthen our wills, that we may pursue the way of reconciliation among our families and communities, in the Spirit of Jesus Christ who pioneered that way.

DESPAIR AND HOPE IN A DARK TIME

Refrain: How long, O God, how long?

WHAT are they now but a name,
the empires of old that have vanished?
What are they now but ruins,
cities that gleamed with pride?
Where will our idolatry end?
How many more succumb to the engines of war?

Warsaw and Dresden, Geurnica and Hamburg,
Hiroshima, Beirut, and Hanoi –
What fury to come from our darkened hearts?
We hanker after the Abyss,
as we and our cities go into the night.

You that wept for Jerusalem,
that knew not what made for its peace,
see now your prophecy extend
as we enter the eclipse of our God.

We stare dumbly at the death camps of hell:
lo! dark Evil is crowned
in the midst of the tortured and dying.
The needy are forgotten,
the oppressed know not the stronghold of God.

The hope of the weary grows dim;
the heavens are empty;
no ear hears the moan of those stricken down
beneath a pitiless sky.

O God, don't you hear the hard-pressed cries?
Have you forgotten? When will you listen?
How long must we endure, how long?

I can no longer praise you for shattering my enemies,
proud of the justice of my cause.
Nor can I claim you for our side,
and urge you to slay them and blot out their name.
We are snared in the work of our own hands:
our own feet are caught in the net that we hid.

But I will not give in to despair,
for you came to your people of old,
in desert and exile, betrayal and death,
giving joy and great hope,
the light of your Presence
in the least expected of places.

Even from the depths of our doom
comes the cry of the victory of God.
Alleluia! Alleluia!

*O God of hope, be with us through the depths of our despair, and work in us the
costly ways of peace, that in justice and gentleness your reign may come on earth.*

THE PLEADING OF THE POOR

Refrain: Remove the sting of the powerful.

WHY do you stand far off, O God, so mute,
hiding yourself from your people in time of our need?
We are pursued by the arrogant rich:
let them be trapped in the schemes of their devising.

They boast of the desires of their hearts:
greedy for gain, they curse and denounce you.
In the pride of their countenance they no longer seek you,
cold-eyed in denial that there is such a God.

And yet their ways prosper:
loftily making their judgments, they scoff at us.
They think in their hearts they will not be disturbed,
through all generations never meeting adversity.

But their mouths are full of deceit and cursing,
under their tongues are oppression and mischief.
They sit in ambush by the forest road:
in city streets they stalk and murder.
Their eyes watch stealthily for the helpless,
they lurk like lions to seize the poor.

The afflicted are crushed, we sink down and fall
under the weight of their scheming devices.
Denied a name, defrauded of land,
we are reduced to a number,
no voice in our destiny.

The powerful think in their hearts, God has forgotten.
God has turned away and will never see.
O God, cry aloud till they hear you:
disturb their conscience, call them to account.

Forget not the afflicted,
do justice to the oppressed and the orphans.
May the powerful strike terror no more.
Break the strength of their arms,
scour out all wickedness from them.

Hear the desire of the poor,
strengthen our hearts.
May the rich denounce their pride and their greed,
the wickedness that brims with excess.

May they see themselves without their fine clothes,
naked and defenceless before you.
We know that we are their judges, O God,
to purge them with truth and refine them with love,
and together be received in your mercy.

*O God, listening and suffering, your silence makes us think you are deaf to our
cries: test our faith and patience no more than we can bear, and be known among
us as the judge of the earth who does right; through Jesus Christ our Saviour.*

THE REPENTANCE OF THE RICH

Refrain: Melt the ice of our hearts,
release the spring of the trap.

In arrogance we rich have pursued the poor:
let us be trapped in the schemes we have devised.
We have boasted of the desires of our hearts:
greedy for gain we have renounced you, O God.

In the pride of our countenance we have not sought you,
cold-eyed in denial we have turned away wilful.
Our ways prospered, our profits increased:
loftily making our judgments, we scoffed at our foes.
We thought in our hearts, We shall not be disturbed,
through all generations not meeting adversity.

Our mouths were full of cursing and scoffing.
Under our tongues were oppression and mischief.
We have sat in ambush in country lanes,
in city streets we have stalked and murdered.
Our eyes have watched stealthily for the helpless,
we lurked like lions to seize the poor.

We crushed the afflicted, they sank down and fell
under the the weight of our frozen hearts.
We denied them a name, defrauded them of land.
We reduced them to a number, no voice in their destiny.
We thought in our hearts, God has forgotten.
God has turned away and will never see.

At last their cry reaches our ears,
we hear the whisper of a conscience revived.
Call us, O God, to account.
Do not forget the ones we afflicted.
Do justice through us to the orphans.

May we strike terror no more.
Break the strength of our arms,
return us to the ways of justice and law.
Hear the desire of the poor:
strengthen their hearts.

We renounce our pride and our greed,
the wickedness that brims with excess.
Defenceless and naked before you,
may we be judged by those we oppressed.
Refine us with fire, purge us with truth,
bring us at last to your mercy.

O God of light and truth, bring us face to face with our weakness and fear, that we may be freed to greet the outcast with love, no longer trampling them under our feet or freezing them out of our hearts. We pray this in the generous laughter of the Spirit of Jesus Christ.

THE PRAYER OF A TREMBLING HEART

*Refrain: As a hazelnut lies in the palm of my hand,
so I rest secure in the presence of God.*

I FEAR the fanatics who toy with the trigger,
oiling their rifles with consummate care,
ready to pounce in the dimly lit alley,
raping the makers of peace and of justice.

But to flee like a bird to the mountains –
no safety in the caves of the earth in our day:
the very foundations are splitting apart,
there is nowhere to go but the place where we are.

I turn again in your presence, dear God,
seeking to renew my trust in your care.
For we tremble and shake, gripped by that fear:
the world we have known is crumbling around us,
invisible rain falls on the mountains,
even the caves of the earth fill with rubble.

Within the future that is coming to meet us,
still are you present with us, O God.
Though you seem so remote in our days,
turning your back, dead to the world,
yet we believe that you hold us in mind,
purging us of violence and hardness of heart,
raining coals of fire in our wickedness,
burning up our fury in your own scorching wind.

Give us new integrity of heart,
renew in us the deeds that you love,
justice and mercy, compassion and courage.
Then face to face shall we see you,
knowing and known, loving and loved.

O God of roaring fire and kindly flame, seeking to harness the wild winds of our winter, burning the decayed, and warming new seeds, steady our hearts, deepen our trust, lead us through to the birth of a new age, in Jesus Christ our Pioneer.

WORDS AND THE WORD

Refrain: *O God, fulfil your promise:*
            let your Word take flesh among us.

WHO speaks any longer the truth of the heart,
words that are clear of corruption and lies?
Neighbour speaks false unto neighbour,
flattery on our lips, deceit in our hearts.
The proud, silver-tongued with smooth words,
control the dumb and the awkward of speech.

O God, cut out the forked tongue, silence the lying lips.
Save us from the corruption of language,
from manipulators of words, greedy for power.
For we drown in menacing lies:
the spring of original falsehood now swells to torrent and spate.

May the exiles and migrants, denied their own language,
find living words to shape their own truth,
words that give meaning to lives without purpose,
that heal and inspire and reach deep in the heart.

Speak to us out of your silence, O God,
our minds purged of gossip and chatter.
For you are the fountain of all that is true,
a wellspring deep that never fails.

It is there that we drink long of your Word,
as sure as a friend who is tested and tried.
For your Promise is true and worthy of trust,
like silver refined in the furnace.

*Spirit of truth, lead us into all truth, and give us the words to speak it, words
that spring deep in the heart and do not distort or betray. We pray this in the name
of the One who lived that truth, Jesus Christ our Saviour.*

THE PAIN OF THE HEART

Refrain: *Warm the pain of my heart,*
               with the lance of your healing.

How long, O God, how long?
You hide your face from me,
you utterly forget me.

How long, O God, how long?
My being is in anguish and torment,
my heart is grieved day and night.

How long, O God, how long?
Icy death, dread and despair,
insidious foes, they strengthen their grip.

Dull are my eyes and lifeless,
as I stare at the desolate places.
Give light to my eyes,
stir up my will and my passion,
my trust in your life-giving Spirit.

Fill my heart with compassion and strength,
that I may rejoice in your generous love,
able to strive with my foes,
no longer dead in the depths of my being.

Yes, at the moment of emptiness and dread
you surprise me with joy and deliverance.
I will sing and shout with delight,
for you have overwhelmed me with grace.

O living loving God, taking to yourself the pains of the world, cherish our wounded hearts in a tender embrace, and cradle our scars, that we may witness to your glory; through the Pain-bearer Christ we pray.

THE FOLLY OF THE RICH

Refrain: *Fill our hearts with compassion,*
          our wills with justice.

LIKE fools we say in our hearts, ''There is no God.''
We have become so vile in our deeds
that no one among us does good.

God searches long among the children of earth
to see if any act wisely,
any who seek to follow the Way.
But we have turned aside from our God,
we are caught in the web of corruption.

There is none that does good, no, not one.
The mists of evil cloud our understanding:
we devour one another like bread,
delighting in the slaughter of peoples:
no longer do we pray to God.
Far from the ways of justice and friendship,
we frustrate the hopes of the poor.

Our hearts will be struck with terror and grief
when we see God saving the poor,
turning their fortune to gladness and joy.

Humble us, O God, our wealth turned to ash;
empty us, that we may be filled with your grace.
Turn our feet into the ways of your justice,
that we may ask forgiveness of those we have wronged.

Then Jacob shall rejoice, and Israel shout for joy,
the whole earth shall sing and be glad,
all the peoples content in their day,
shrivelled seeds warmed by the poor,
the wealthy led at last to the dance.

O God of the poor, prune our lives of all that we cling to. O Spirit of true wealth, draw us through the narrow gate of loss. O Christ who lives in those we neglect, through their generosity turn us to repentance, that we may be forgiven.

FRIENDS OF GOD

Refrain: *Friend of God, deepen your Spirit within us,*
              for you laid down your life for your friends.

DEAR God, who are the honoured guests in your tent?
Who may dwell in your presence upon your holy mountain?
Who may commune with those who are your heart's desire,
lovingly embraced in the union of friends?

Those who lead uncorrupt lives,
and do the thing that is right,
who speak the truth from their hearts,
and have not slandered with their tongue.

Those who have not betrayed their friends,
nor rained down abuse on their neighbours,
in whose eyes the shifty have no honour,
but hold in high esteem those who fear God.

Those who give their word to their neighbour,
and do not go back on their promise,
who have not grown wealthly at the expense of the poor,
nor grown sleek with flattery and bribes.

Those who recognize the outcast as the one whom they need,
who forgive to seventy times seven,
who depend on the mercy of God,
and live the highest law that is love.

Those who are steadfast and kind,
who are resilient and patient and humble,
who know the cost of a morsel of justice,
a glimpse of compassion in times that are savage.

Their roots are deep in the being of God,
their arms are spread wide in welcome embrace.
They are faithful, joyful, and blessed,
God's sisters and brothers and friends.

Loving God, whose name is Friendship, so guide us in your Spirit that we may embrace the way that finds joy in giving all for others, so that even our enemies may become our friends, after the pattern of Jesus of Nazareth who loved his own even to the end.

PRAYER FOR THE DEPARTED

Refrain: *Greet them in the joy of your presence.*

O GOD our refuge and strength,
preserve us from lasting harm.
Again and again we affirm,
in times both of doubt and of trust,
You are our faithful Creator,
in you alone is our bliss.

We thank you for all your holy people,
all whose lives give you glory.
We praise you for your martyrs and saints,
in whom you take great delight.

As for those held in highest esteem,
those idols adored by the crowd,
those gods they fête and run after,
we will not take their name on our lips.
They are bloated with pride and success,
punctured by thorns in the late autumn wind.

Your name alone do we praise,
our resting place now and for ever.
You feed us with the Bread of Life,
you nourish us with the Cup of Salvation.

We have been so fortunate in our days,
and in the places were we have lived.
To no one else belongs the praise,
but to you, the great Giver of gifts.

We give you thanks for the wisdom of your counsel,
even at night you have instructed our hearts.
In the silence of the darkest of hours
we open our ears to the whisper of your voice.

Refrain: *Greet them in the joy of your presence.*

We have set your face always before us,
in every cell of our being you are there.
As we tremble on the narrowest of paths,
the steadying of your hand gives us courage.
Fleet of foot, with our eyes on the goal,
headlong in the chasm we shall not fall.

Therefore our hearts rejoice and our spirits are glad,
our whole being shall rest secure.
For you will not give us over to the power of death,
nor let your faithful one see the pit.

You will show us the path of life:
in your countenance is the fulness of joy.
From the spring of your heart flow rivers of delight,
a fountain of water that shall never run dry.

O God of the living, keep our eyes fixed on the goal of our journey, that we may be fleet of heart, and in all our dyings leap to the embrace of the One who lures us with love, the pioneer of our salvation, Jesus, our elder brother and faithful friend.

AN ANGRY CRY FOR JUSTICE

Refrain: *Take the sword, O God, from our hands,*
           wield it with truth and with healing.
           Let justice roll down like waters,
           righteousness like an ever-flowing stream.

HEAR my cause, O God, for it is just:
listen to my prayer from lips that do not lie.
Let judgment come forth from your presence:
let your eyes discern what is right.
Though you test me by fire,
and search my heart in the dark of night,
you will find no wickedness in me.
My mouth is not that of the deceiver,
I have kept true to your Word.
My steps have held firm to your paths,
my feet have not stumbled.

I call upon you, O God, for you will answer:
incline your ear to me, and hear my words.
Show me the wonders of your steadfast love,
O Saviour of those who come to you for refuge.
By your right hand you deliver them
from the deadly grip of those who surround them.
Keep me as the apple of an eye,
hide me under the shadow of your wings
from the onslaught of the wicked,
from my enemies encircling me to put me in chains.
They have closed their hearts to pity:
their mouths speak pride and arrogance.
They track me down and surround me on every side,
watching how to bring me to the ground.
They are like lions greedy for their prey,
like young lions lurking in ambush.

Refrain: *Take the sword, O God, from our hands,*
              wield it with truth and with healing.
              Let justice roll down like waters,
              righteousness like an ever-flowing stream.

Though I trust I am safe in your presence, O God,
yet do I fear, there is terror in my heart.
Arise, stand in their way and cast them down:
deliver me from the wicked by your sword.
Slay them with your iron fist,
slay them that they perish from the earth,
destroy them from among the living.
May they choke on the grapes of your wrath,
let their bellies be filled with maggots.
May their children never come of age,
their heritage dying with them.
As for me, I shall see your face because my cause is just:
when I awake and see you as you are, I shall be satisfied.

O God, like the psalmist of old I am angry
at the ways of the brutal on earth.
Afraid of their cruelty and greed,
I tremble on the point of their sword.
Yet the hammer of my words and my cries
is held in my hands, poised in the air.
For I know the evil in my own heart,
the lying, the pride, and the arrogance.
Purge me of self-righteousness and hatred,
of smugness and satisfied smile.
Help me to love my enemies with truth,
for we are all children of your love.
Even as I pray for your justice,
for the vindication of your promise,
that oppressors may triumph no more,
that their victims may run free in the wind,
so I pray for my deliverance too.
Save us through judgment and mercy,
dependent as we are on your faithfulness.

O God, compassionate and just, wielder of the one sword that pierces with truth and healing, penetrate the murk and fury of our hearts, that our anger may be shaped by the power of your Spirit, that we may create with you that Commonwealth of Justice and of Peace that is yours alone, and for which we pray through Jesus Christ our Saviour.

RESCUE

Refrain: *Praise to the God of compassion and love,*
            the power that rescues and saves.

I LOVE you, O God my strength,
my crag, my fortress, and my deliverer,
the rock to which I cling for refuge,
my shield, my saviour, and my stronghold.
I called to you with loud lamentation,
and you sprang the trap which held me fast.

The waves of death swept over my head,
the floods of chaos surged around me.
The cord of the grave tightened about my neck,
the snares of death sprang shut in my path.
In my anguish I called to you, O God:
I cried in desperation for your help.

Your ear was closer to me than I thought:
you heard me from the depths of my heart.
Then did it seem that the earth was quaking:
the foundations of the hills were shaken:
they trembled because of the power of your anger.

Down you came like a dragon,
swooping on the wings of the wind.
Smoke went forth from your nostrils,
and a consuming fire from your mouth.
You parted the heavens and came down,
riding upon the cherubim,
thick darkness under your feet.
Your voice roared through the heavens,
sharp arrows of lightning,
roll upon roll of thunder,
laying bare the foundations of the world.

Like an eagle you swooped down and took me,
lifting me from the jaws of the sea.
You delivered me from all that imprisoned me,
from those I thought stronger than I.
They fell upon me in the day of calamity,
yet you rescued me and led me to safety.
You brought me into a broad place,
you gave me freedom because you delight in me.

I deserve no reward for anything I have done,
no recompense for the cleanness of my hands.
Have I kept to your ways, O God,
and not turned aside to do evil?
Was my eye always on your command,
did I take your wisdom to my heart?
I dare claim no innocence in your presence,
corrupt have been the deeds of my hands.

Yet still you delight in me – I am astonished –
loving and pursuing the one you are creating,
yearning for me to live in your image.
You are faithful even when I betray you,
when I feel the wrath of your love.
You carefully smooth out my crookedness,
forgiving my sin and wrongdoing.

Such are the faces of your Love,
each reflected in the pool of my being.
For you will save a humble people,
and bring down the high looks of the proud.
You light a lamp for my path,
you make my darkness to be bright.
With your help I can meet all that comes,
with the help of my God I can face evil's defences.

Refrain: *Praise to the God of compassion and love,*
              the power that rescues and saves.

O God, your Way is perfect,
your Word has been tried in the fire.
You are a shield to all who trust in you.
You are my rock and I hold to you.
You gird me with strength
and make my way safe before me.
You make my feet like the feet of the deer,
you set me surefooted on the mountain path.

You teach my hands to fight,
and my arm to aim true with an arrow.
You have given me the shield of salvation;
your right hand guides and supports me.
Your swift response has made me great:
you lengthen my stride beneath me,
and my feet do not slip.

I pursue my enemies and overtake them,
striving till they cease their rebellion.
I fight them till they surrender their arms,
stumbling and falling before me.
Wild in their panic they stagger,
and cry out for mercy and help.
Tempted as I am to be cruel,
to beat them fine as dust in the wind,
to cast them out like the mire of the streets,
yet in your mercy I spare them.
In my struggle with them you deliver me,
and people I had not known become your servants.
Their strength of resistance withers away,
they come trembling from the last of their strongholds.

I cannot ignore the evil in my ways,
however loyal I have been to your covenant.
I cannot deny the good in my enemies,
however hidden and obscured from my sight.
Though I must strive to put an end to their power,
humbly believing that their evil is monstrous –
for no longer do they see their victims as human,
they see only the power of missile and jet –
yet I resist evil means to disarm them,
refusing to treat them as numbers.
O God, renew in us your covenant of peace,
a promise that you gave to all peoples:
desperate is the need of our day.

God lives! God reigns!
Blessed be the rock of my salvation!
Those who set themselves against you have been subdued,
you have set me free from their grip,
delivering me from days of violence and bloodshed.
For this I give you thanks among the people,
and sing praises to your name.
Great love do you show to those whom you care for,
great triumph in fulfilling your purpose of glory,
keeping faith with David your servant,
with his descendants in flesh and in faith.

*O Saviour God, lead us through the taut place of our despair, that we may emerge
into a land broad and free, through Jesus Christ crucified and risen.*

THE LOVE THAT MOVES THE STARS

Refrain: *Praise to the Love that moves the stars,*
                   and stirs in the depths of our hearts.

THE web of the world trembles,
the whisper of a great wind passing.
The caressing of strings makes music,
its sighs reach the ends of the world.

The stars in the heavens chant the glory of God,
pulsing their praise across aeons of space.
From the soft radiance of a summer dawn
to the stormy sunset of a winter's evening,
from the darkest and wildest of mountain nights
to the stillness of moonlit seas,
the voice of praise is never silent,
yet all without speech or language
or sound of any voice.

So too with the mighty sun,
come forth as a bridegroom from his tent,
rejoicing at his wedding day,
exulting in youthful splendour and beauty.
He climbs the sky from the eastern horizon,
he declines to the west at the end of the day,
and nothing can escape the fire of his presence.

Galaxies beyond take up the cry,
suns every more brilliant and huge:
Arcturus twenty times the size of Earth's sun,
Sigma in Dorado hundreds of thousands,
Aldebaran millions of miles in diameter,
Alpha in Lyre three hundred thousand light years away:
all, all proclaim the glory of God.

The law of God is perfect, refreshing the soul,
the words of God are sure, and give wisdom to the simple.
The justice of God is righteous, and rejoices the heart,
the commandment of God is pure, and gives light to the eyes.
The fear of God is clean, and endures for ever,
the judgments of God are true, and just in every way.

So they dance as the stars of the universe,
perfect as the parabolas of comets,
like satellites and planets in their orbits,
reliable and constant in their courses.

The Wisdom of God – more to be desired than gold,
sweeter than syrup and honey from the comb.
And by her is your servant taught,
in the very keeping of her there is great reward.

Who can tell how often I offend?
Cleanse me from my secret faults.
Keep your servant from pride and conceit,
lest they get the dominion over me.
So may I stand in your presence,
innocent of great offence.
Let the words of my mouth
and the meditations of my heart,
be always acceptable in your sight,
O God, my strength and my redeemer.

*Creator God, yearning and striving to bring harmony out of chaos, so fill with
your Wisdom the inscape of our being, and so move with the Wind of your
presence among the landscapes of our world, that the Earth may reflect the glory
and wonder of the universe, transfigured in the image of Jesus Christ, at one with
you in the cost of creating.*

A PRAYER FOR THOSE WHO GOVERN

Refrain: *Give your Spirit of wisdom and justice*
to those who govern and lead.

GOD of Abraham and Sarah, God of our ancestors,
creating among us your realm and your glory,
bless those who rule on the people's behalf,
give them strength in time of our troubles.

Send them the help of your light and your wisdom,
give them support through the prayers of our hearts.
Remember their promise to serve all the people,
take from them their lust for power and for wealth.

Remember our promise to serve others' good,
accept the sacrifice of lives that are broken.
Give to your people the desire of their hearts,
fulfilling within them all that they cherish.

We shout for joy for your blessings towards us,
we lift high the Cross in the name of our God.
For you saved us with the power of unbroken love,
and indeed you fulfil what we deeply desire.

May the rulers of the people acknowledge your name,
serve the common good in the light of your justice.
Some put their trust in weapons of war,
but we shall trust in the power of your name.
They will decay, rust and collapse,
but those strong in God will endure through the days.

May those who lead us trust you, O God.
Give them wisdom to lead through laws that are just.
For you will answer our prayer in the day of our cry,
fulfilling your nature and your own lasting name.

Wise and compassionate One, guide those who bear office in public life, that they
may use their power for the common good, in village, town, and city, in this and
every land; through Jesus Christ our Servant-Lord.

ROYAL PRIESTHOOD

Refrain: *To God be the glory: alleluia!*

It is your royal road, O God,
it is your sovereign way –
to lead in the spirit of service,
to be stewards in your household,
to be guardians one for another,
to guide others in your paths.

As monarchs rejoice in your strength,
so may we exult in your help.
As the sovereign trusts in your faithfulness,
so do we rely on your steadfastness.

You have given us our heart's desire,
even the gift of your justice and wisdom.
You came to meet us with goodly blessings,
and placed crowns of gold on our heads.
We asked you for life and you gave it us,
long days of contentment in your presence.

You have destined even us for glory,
clothing us with splendour and honour.
You have promised us everlasting felicity,
and made us glad with the joy of your presence.

By your light we shall penetrate the dark,
striving till they yield with our enemies.
All that is evil will wither at your coming,
as the chaff is consumed in the fire.
Those who stir malice will be overwhelmed,
their plots of mischief will come to nothing.

No longer will their infection spread through the years,
to the third and the fourth generations.
You will put all their scheming to flight,
stunning them with a glance from your eye.

Refrain: *To God be the glory: alleluia!*

Be exalted, O God, in your strength,
the power of your love and your truth,
your wisdom and your justice for ever:
we shall sing for joy and praise your name.

Sovereign of the universe, who has destined even us for glory, with crowns upon our heads, enable us in your Spirit to serve one another with justice, that none may be the victim of exploitation and violence, of cruelty and greed; we pray this in the name of Jesus Christ, the Poor Man of Nazareth.

WHY? WHY? WHY?

Refrain for Part One: Why, silent God, why?

My God, my God, why have you forsaken me?
Why are you so far from helping me?
O my God, I howl in the daytime but you do not hear me.
I groan in the watches of the night, but I find no rest.

Yet still you are the holy God whom Israel long has worshipped.
Our ancestors hoped in you, and you rescued them.
They trusted in you, and you delivered them.
They called upon you: you were faithful to your covenant.
They put their trust in you and were not disappointed.

But as for me, I crawl the earth like a worm,
despised by others, an outcast of the people.
All those who see me laugh me to scorn:
they make mouths at me, shaking their heads and saying,
"He threw himself on God for deliverance:
let God rescue him then, if God so delights in him."

You were my midwife, O God, drawing me out of the womb.
I was weak and unknowing, yet you were my hope –
even as I lay close to the breast,
cast upon you from the days of my birth.
From the womb of my mother to the dread of these days,
you have been my God, never letting me go.

Do not desert me, for trouble is hard at hand,
and there is no one to help me.
Wild beasts close in on me, narrow-eyed, greedy and sleek.
They open their mouths and snarl at me, like a ravening and
    roaring lion.

Refrain for Part One: *Why, silent God, why?*

My strength drains away like water, my bones are out of joint.
My heart also in the midst of my body is even like melting wax.
My mouth is dried up like a potsherd, my tongue cleaves to my
　　gums.
My hands and my feet are withered, you lay me down in the
　　dust of death.

The huntsmen are all about me:
a circle of wicked men hem me in on every side,
their dogs unleashed to tear me apart.
They have pierced my hands and my feet –
I can count all my bones –
they stand staring and gloating over me.
They divide my garments among them
they cast lots for my clothes.

The tanks of the mighty encircle me,
barbed wire and machine guns surround me.
They have marked my arm with a number,
and never call me by name.
They have stripped me of clothes and of shoes,
and showered me with gas in the chamber of death.

I cry out for morphine but no one hears me.
Pinned down by straitjacket I scream the night through.
I suffocate through panic in the oxygen tent.
Sweating with fear, I await news of my doom.

No one comes near with an unmasked face,
no skin touches mine in a gesture of love.
They draw back in terror, speaking only
in whispers behind doors that are sealed.

Be not far from me, O God: you are my helper, hasten to my aid.
Deliver my very self from the sword, my life from the falling of
　　the axe.
Save me from the mouth of the lion,
poor body that I am, from horns of the bull.

Silent God, we bring the cries of our battered hearts, and the cries of those burdened by illness and bowed down by the weight of oppression. We bring them so that we may not be silent. Hear us in the name of Jesus, forsaken on the Cross.

Refrain for Part Two: *Even though you slay me,*
                           yet will I trust you.

I WILL declare your name to my friends:
in the midst of the congregation I will praise you.
We stand in awe of you and bow down before you,
we glorify and magnify your name.

For you have not shrunk in loathing
from the suffering in their affliction.
You have not hid your face from them,
but when they called to you, you heard them.

My praise is of you in the great congregation,
my vows I will perform in their sight.
We shall praise you with thanksgiving and wonder.
We shall share what we have with the poor:
they shall eat and be satisfied,
a new people, yet to be born.
Those who seek you shall be found by you:
they will be in good heart for ever.

So shall my life be preserved in your sight,
and my children shall worship you:
they shall tell of you to generations yet to come:
to a people yet to be born
they shall declare your righteousness,
that you have brought these things to fulfilment.

So let all the ends of the world remember
and turn again to their God.
Let all the families of the nations worship their Creator.
For all dominion belongs to you,
  and you are the ruler of the peoples.

*O God of enduring love, whom the clouds obscure, may our eye of faith turn
steadily towards you, patiently waiting in hope for the fulness of your salvation,
bearing the pain of evil days, in Jesus of the Cross, who loved his own even to the
end, and who kept on trusting even when there was no answer to his cry.*

Refrain for Part Three: *We trust in the folly of the Cross.*

CAN we now hold on to such faith?
Has the name of God become an offence to our ears?
Is God deaf to the cry of the child,
offering no relief to the burning of pain,
letting the horror of life run wild,
sitting lofty and high, refusing to act?

So do we argue and wrestle in faith,
fiercely refusing to loosen our hold.
We demand that you listen to whisper and howl,
that your deeds may fulfil your nature and name.

This is our story from Jeremiah and Job,
from all who find you obscure and perplexing.
Who are you? Who do you say that you are?
Why must we be buffeted by malice and chance?

Is our cry no more than our pride?
Is our mind too small? Is our eye too dim?
Do not quiet our pain with dazzling display.
The open wound of the child accuses you still.

Is there a cry in the depths of your being,
in the heart and soul of your chosen Christ-Self?
Stretched between earth and the heavens,
we see a striving so awesome,
a strange and harrowing love,
a bearing of pain between father and son,
a loving right through to the end,
through the worst of devil and death.

Truly you are an offence, O God,
and scandalous too are the outcries of faith.
They bite deep into the lines of our faces,
as we strive to be faithful and true.
Keep us from the scandal of hypocrisy,
selfish and faithless, prayers merely mouthed,
so far from the Place of the Skull,
too indifferent to be in conflict with you,
too icily cold for your friendship.

Refrain for Part Three: *We trust in the folly of the Cross.*

Today if you hear the voice of *this* God,
your heart need no longer be hardened.

O God of the Cross, keep us passionate through our wrestling with your ways, and keep us humble before the mystery of your great love, known to us in the face of Jesus Christ.

Refrain for Part Four: *In the depths of our darkness*
you are rising, O Christ.

AND can those who are buried give you worship,
those ground to the dust give you praise?
Will nothing be left but the wind and the silence,
a dead earth, abandoned, forgotten?

But you are a God who creates out of nothing,
you are a God who raises the dead,
you are a God who redeems what is lost,
you are a God who fashions new beauty,
striving with the weight of your glory,
bearing the infinite pain.

The footfalls of faith may drag through our days,
God's gift of a costly and infinite enduring.
We remember your deliverance of your people of old,
we remember the abundance of the earth you have given us,
we remember the care and compassion of folk,
we remember your victory of long-suffering love.

The power of the powers is but a feather in the wind!
Death is transfigured to glory for ever!

Risen Christ, breaking the bonds of death, shine on us with eyes of compassion
and glory. Let light flood the dungeons of our rejected and downtrodden selves.
So may the oppressed go free, the weak rise up in strength, and the hungry be fed,
now in these our days.

THE SHEPHERD AND THE HOST

Refrain: Dwell in me that I may dwell in you.

DEAR God, you sustain me and feed me:
like a shepherd you guide me.
You lead me to an oasis of green,
to lie down by restful waters.

Quenching my thirst, you restore my life:
renewed and refreshed, I follow you,
a journey on the narrowest of paths.
You keep me true to your name.

Even when cliffs loom out of the mist,
my step is steady because of my trust.
Even when I go through the deepest valley,
with the shadow of darkness and death,
I will fear no evil or harm.
For you are with me to give me strength,
your crook, your staff, at my side.

Even in the midst of my troubles,
with the murmurs of those who disturb me,
I know I can feast in your presence.

You spread a banquet before me,
you anoint my head with oil,
you stoop to wash my feet,
you fill my cup to the brim.

Your loving kindness and mercy
will meet me every day of my life.
By your Spirit you dwell within me,
and in the whole world around me,
and I shall abide in your house,
content in your presence for ever.

Wise and loving Shepherd, you guide your people in the ways of your truth, leading us through the waters of baptism and nourishing us with the food of eternal life: keep us in your mercy, and so guide us through the perils of evil and death, that we may know your joy at the heart of all things, both now and for ever.

THE GLORY OF GOD

Refrain: *Praise to the Glory of God,*
            shining through Jesus Christ.

DEAR God, you are creating the earth and all that is in it,
the whole round world and all who dwell on land or sea.
You have founded life upon the waters,
and drawn it forth from the mysterious deeps.

Who shall climb the mountain of God?
Who shall stand in the holy place?
Those who have clean hands and pure hearts,
who have not set their minds on falsehood,
nor sworn to deceive their neighbours.
They shall receive a blessing from God,
and justice from the God of their salvation.
Such is the fortune of those who draw near their Creator,
who seek the face of the God of Jacob.

Let the gates be opened, let the doors be lifted high,
that the great procession may come in.
Who is the One clothed with glory?
It is our God, the God who has triumphed,
who has striven with evil and prevailed.

Let the gates be opened, let the doors be lifted high,
that the great procession may come in.
Who is the One clothed with glory?
It is the great God of all the universe,
glorious in a Love that never fails.

May the light and love of God shine in our hearts and through the universe that the whole creation may be transfigured to glory, in and through Jesus Christ, radiant in the splendour of the wounds of love.

A PRAYER OF THE LONELY

Refrain: *You are the source of my faith,*
             you are the goal of my hope.

O GOD, the foundation of my hope,
you are the gound of my trust.
May I not be disappointed in my days,
may the powers of oppression fade away.

Let none who wait for your coming
turn away with empty hands.
But let those who break faith
be confounded and gain nothing.

Show me your ways, O God,
and teach me your paths.
Lead me in your truth and guide me,
for you are the God of my salvation.

I have hoped in you all the day long,
because of your goodness and faithfulness,
your steadfast love to your people,
streaming towards us from days of old.

Remember not the sins of my youth,
nor my trespass and trampling on others.
According to your mercy think on me,
call to mind your agelong compassion.

You are full of justice and grace:
you guide sinners in the Way.
You lead the humble to do what is right,
filled with the gentle strength of the meek.
All your paths are faithful and true,
for those who are loyal to your covenant.

For your name's sake, O God,
be merciful to me, for my sin is great.
I come to you in trembling and awe:
guide me in the way I should choose.

Refrain: *You are the source of my faith,*
            you are the goal of my hope.

I shall be at home with what is right,
I shall dwell at ease in the land.
My children shall be stewards after me,
your creation cared for in days yet to come.
Your friendship is your gift to me,
revealed in the keeping of your covenant.

My eyes look towards you, O God,
and you free me from the snares of the net.
Turn your face to me –
it is full of your grace and your love.

For I am lonely and in misery,
my heart is in pain and constricted:
the arteries of affection are hardened.
Open me wide and lift my heart high,
the breath of your Spirit filling my lungs.
Take to yourself my wretched affliction,
bring me out of my distress,
and forgive me all my sins.

See how strong are the powers of oppression,
eyes full of hatred and violence.
Guard my life and deliver me,
clothe me with integrity and love.

Bring me to the innocence that no longer harms,
for you are my strength and salvation.
I wait for you: you are my hope;
may I never shrink away in shame.

*Compassionate and loving God, take from me the burden of self-hatred, the
whisper of loathing that says I am worthless. Fill me with the spirit of forgiveness
and grace, that I may deeply accept that I am accepted just as I am, in Jesus
Christ the Beloved of your Heart.*

INNOCENT OR GUILTY?

Refrain for Part One: *We give you thanks, O God,*
                             for you make your people righteous.

GIVE judgment for me, O God,
for I have walked in my integrity,
I have trusted you without wavering.

Put me to the test and try me,
examine my mind and my heart.
For your steadfast love is before my eyes,
and I have walked in your truth.

I have not sat with deceivers,
nor consorted with hypocrites;
I hate the company of evildoers,
and I will not sit with the wicked.

I wash my hands in innocence, O God,
that I may approach your altar,
lifting up the voice of thanksgiving,
and telling of all your marvellous deeds.

Dear God, I love the house of your dwelling,
the place where your glory shines.
Do not sweep me away with sinners,
nor my life with people of blood,
who murder with their evil weapons,
and whose hands are full of bribes.

As for me I walk in my integrity:
redeem me and be gracious to me.
My foot stands on firm ground:
I will bless you in the great congregation.

Refrain for Part Two: Kyrie eleison
                                  Christe eleison
                                  Kyrie eleison

WHO in this world of ours now
dare take that prayer as their own?
Perhaps the ones imprisoned for conscience,
persecuted and tortured for faith,
tempted to renounce their beliefs,
holding firm to the most sacred of vows.
Yet even the greatest of saints
knows no boast in the presence of God.

Forgive the boast of your people, O God,
self-righteous and blind in our mouthings.
We have not done a tenth of these things,
nor dare we plead any innocence.
We project the evil of our hearts on to others,
and destroy our enemies in your cause.
The drumbeat of the psalmist has sounded
through years of inquisitions and wars.

*We pray for the enemy, in others and in ourselves, the one who whispers the lie
and imprisons the tellers of truth. O God, forgive our laziness, our fear, our
stupidity, and shed on us the painful healing beams of the light of Jesus Christ
the living Truth.*

COURAGEOUS FAITH IN TURBULENT TIMES

Refrain: *In time of disquiet and trouble,*
with courage will I trust you, O God.

GOD is my light and my salvation:
whom then shall I fear?
God is the strength of my life:
of whom then shall I be afraid?
In God alone do I put my trust:
how then can others harm me?

When the wicked, even my enemies,
come upon me to devour me,
they stumble and fall back.
When a mighty army is laid against me,
my heart shall not be afraid.
When war rises up against me,
yet will I put my trust in God.

One thing have I desired of God
that I will seek after,
even that I may dwell in the house of my God
all the days of my life,
to feast my eyes on the beauty of my Creator,
to ponder deeply the gracious will of my God.

In the time of my trouble
you will hide me in your shelter;
in the shadow of your tent
you will conceal me
from those who pursue me;
high on a pinnacle of rock
you will place me safe
from those who surge around me.

Therefore I will offer in your dwelling place
gifts with great gladness:
I will sing and praise your name.

Refrain: *In time of disquiet and trouble,*
          with courage will I trust you, O God.

Listen to me, O God, when I cry to you:
have mercy upon me and be gracious to me.
Do not hide your face from me,
nor cast your servant away in your anger.

The voice of my heart has impelled me:
Seek the face of the living God.
Out of the darkness I discern your presence
in the face of the Risen Christ,
revealing your pain and your joy
in new and abundant life.

Indeed you have been my helper,
you have not forsaken me, O God of my salvation.
Though my family and friends may desert me,
you will sustain me in the power of the Risen One.

Guide me in your way and lead me on your path.
So in the joy of your presence I can meet my adversaries,
even when false witnesses rise up against me,
or those who do me violence and wrong.

I should have utterly fainted but that I truly believe
I shall see your goodness in the land of the living.
I shall patiently wait for your good time:
I put my trust in our faithful Creator:
I shall be strong and let my heart take courage.

In all these things we are more than conquerors
through Christ who loved us.
For I am sure that neither death nor life,
nor angels nor principalities nor powers,
nor things present nor things to come,
nor height nor depth, nor anything else in all creation,
will be able to separate us from the love of God
in Christ Jesus our Servant-Lord and our Saviour.

Creator God, faithful to your covenant with the earth, steady our hearts and wills in these times of great turbulence, that we may in deed fulfil your purpose for us as heralds of your just and lasting peace; through Jesus Christ our Saviour.

THE SILENCE AND THE VOICE

Refrain: *Come, Wind of the Spirit,*
              with the Voice of our God.

DEAR God, are you the Friend I can trust?
You seem so deaf to my prayer,
to the urgent sound of my voice.
Do you not hear, do you turn away silent,
when I cry out for help?
I lift up my hands in the holy place,
but still I hear no answer.

Let me pause and remember
the holy ground of your presence –
the bush burning with light
at the moment of despair.

You are here in the ones I ignore:
the shuffling old man in the street,
the hollow-eyed woman unkempt,
the neighbour I pass hurriedly by.

I see neither their need nor mine,
it is I who turn silent away.
I collude with the ways of wickedness,
speaking peace with my lips,
unaware of the mischief of my heart.
No wonder I do not hear your voice.
I turn away from your presence,
pulled down by my selfish desires.

Open our eyes that we may see,
unblock our ears that we may hear.
Send us the fury of the desert wind,
or the gentle breeze through the trees.
Whether by shouting or whisper,
face us with dark truths of our ways.

No reward dare we claim,
no generosity from your heart.
No wonder we fall in the midst of our devices,
to be built up in strength no more.

And yet there are times of our passion,
our anger at the traps of the poor,
of those without power or numbers.
The voice of the voiceless is heard in our land,
and the sound of your rejoicing, O God.
You are the strength of our hands
as we strive with the powers for your truth.
Our hearts trust you and we thank you,
we dance for joy and with songs give you praise.

Save your people, bless your heritage,
be our shepherd and guard us.
Protect us and bear with us,
both now and for ever.

Remove from our hearts, O God, our apathy and fear, and give us the Spirit of love and freedom, that we may give passionately of ourselves in companionship with the poor and oppressed, and so serve your just and holy rule, revealed to us in Jesus Christ our Liberator.

AWE IN THE PRESENCE OF POWER

Refrain: *Giving voice to the cry of creation,*
we shout Glory to God in the Highest.

LET all the powers of the universe praise the Creator,
ascribing to God glory and strength.
In the beauty of holiness we worship you, O God,
giving you the honour due to your name.

Your voice rolls over the waters,
your glory thunders over the oceans.
Your voice resounds through the mountains,
echoing glory and splendour.

Your voice splits even the cedar trees,
breaking in pieces the cedars of Lebanon.
The trees of the mountainside howl in your wind,
uprooted like matchsticks in the roar of your passing.

Your voice divides the lightning flash,
flames of fire come from your tongue.
Your voice whirls the sands of the desert,
the whistling sands of the desert storm.

Your voice makes the oaks shake and shudder,
and strips the forest bare,
and all in your presence cry, Glory!

O God, more powerful than tempest and flood,
reigning over all your creation,
stillness in the eye of the storm,
give strength to your people in awe of you,
give your people the blessing of peace.

Awesome God, your Love embraces all the powers of creation, and in the presence
of Love we need never be afraid. Give us steadiness and courage and skill to strive
with the energies you have placed in our hands, that the wise use of heat and light,
of atom and laser, may enable the earth and its peoples to flourish and prosper,
according to your will shown to us in Jesus Christ, true image of you, our Creator.

THE TWO CONVERSIONS

Refrain for Part One: *With gentle hand you raise me,*
                                  from death you call me to life.

FROM the depths of despair I cried out,
seared with pain and with grief.
Where are you, O God?
How long must I suffer?

You drew me up from the deeps,
like a prisoner out of a dungeon,
a flesh-body touched by your hand,
flickering and trembling with life.

You brought me out of a land full of gloom,
a place of hollow silence and cold.
You melted my paralyzed fear:
the warmth of your Sun coursed through my veins.

The wrath of your Love lasts but a moment,
for a lifetime your mercy and healing.
Heaviness and weeping last through the night,
yet day breaks into singing and joy.

I will praise you, O God,
for you have made me whole.
I will give you thanks
in the midst of your people.

Refrain for Part Two: *When my feet stumble and stray,*
                          your hand steadies and guides me.

In the strength you gave me I felt secure,
built upon rock, firm as the hills.
Basking in the warmth of your favour,
the prosperity of my days increased.

I slipped into the worship of money,
the goods of this world ensnaring me.
They gathered like a turbulent cloud,
blotting out the sight of your face.

Then I was greatly dismayed,
feeling foolish in toppling pride,
unable to praise you from the wasteland of hell,
to proclaim your name from the graveyards of death.

O God, have mercy upon me,
forgive my self-satisfied pride,
disentangle the web I have woven,
patiently probe me with the scalpel of truth.

You turn my lamentation into dancing,
lifting me to my feet, clothing me with joy.
In the depths of my being I explode into laughter,
and sing with gratitude the triumph of Love.

*Living Christ, look on us with eyes of compassion; call us with the word of
forgiveness, again and again, to seventy times seven, that we may at last hear and
see, and turn our stricken and wounded faces, and know ourselves accepted and
embraced, loved beyond measure and without reserve.*

A PRAYER FOR DELIVERANCE

Refrain: *In the midst of struggle and pain*
we trust in the Love that endures.

I AM bowed down by the heat of battle;
exhausted I limp back to my tent.
Here is my shelter, my refuge,
the place where I know God is with me.
Deliver me, rescue me, redeem me,
for you are just, and swift to save.
You are a stream of refreshment, an oasis of shade;
you give me manna in the wilderness, ever drawing me on.

Lead me and guide me for the sake of your name:
deliver me out of the nets that entangle me,
for you alone are my strength.
Into your hands I cast my whole being,
knowing that you will redeem me,
O God of salvation and truth.

I hate those who cling to vain idols,
for my trust is in you, living God.
I will be glad and rejoice in your love,
for you have seen my affliction,
and soothed my distress.
You have not abandoned me to the power of my enemy:
you have set my feet in a broad place,
where I may walk at liberty.

Have mercy on me, O God,
for I am distressed and in pain:
no one hears the cry of my loneliness.
My eyes have become dimmed with grief,
the whole of me body and soul.

My life is worn away with sorrow,
and my years with mourning.
My strength fails me because of my affliction,
and my bones are wasting away.

I am the scorn of all my enemies,
and a burden to my neighbours.
My acquaintances, they are afraid of me,
shrinking away from my sight.

I am clean forgotten,
like a dead man out of mind.
I have become like a broken vessel.
For I hear the conspiring of many,
the whispering of threats on every side,
as they plot to take away my life.

The hope of my days is in your hands:
I trust you, my God, Thou that art Thou.
Deliver me from the power of my enemies,
from the grip of those who persecute me.
Show your servant the light of your countenance,
and save me in your steadfast love.

Let me not be confounded, O God,
for I have called upon your name.
Let all ungodliness be put to confusion,
and brought to silence in the grave.
Let lying lips be made dumb,
the voices of cruelty and pride
that speak with spite against the just.

How great is your goodness towards us,
poured out on the just and the unjust,
saving us from whisperings within,
from the betrayals of hearts that are frightened,
sheltering us in your refuge
from the strife of tongues.

O God, I give you thanks
for you have shown me marvellous great kindness.
When I was alarmed, like a city besieged,
I felt cut off from your sight.
Nevertheless, you heard the voice of my prayer,
when I cried to you for help.

All your servants love you, O God,
for you enfold us in your faithfulness,
and retrieve us sternly when we are proud.
With firmness of will and courage of heart,
we will follow your way,
trusting that you are our God,
our faithful Creator and Friend.

Living God, faithful to your covenants, loyal to your people, deepen our trust in your loving purposes for all humankind, that we may come to no lasting harm. We pray this in and through Jesus Christ our Redeemer.

RELEASE FROM THE BURDEN OF SIN

Refrain: *Lift my burdens from my shoulders,*
for the yoke of your Love is light.

BLESSED are those whose sin is forgiven,
the trace of whose trespass is erased.
Blessed are those whom God does not blame,
in whose heart is no guile.

I kept my secret sins to myself,
I refused to bring them to the light.
My energy wasted away,
my days were full of complaint,
a grumble murmuring in my ears.
Day and night your hand was heavy upon me:
the flow of my being became sluggish and dry,
like parched land in the drought of summer.

Then I acknowledged my sin in your presence:
I hid no longer from myself or from you.
I said, ''I will confess my evil to God.''
So you released me from the guilt of my sin.

For this cause all those who are faithful
pray in their hearts in the day of their troubles.
Even in times of overwhelming distress,
with the thunder and force of waters in flood,
your grace is for me like a temple of rock,
standing firm in the face of the powers,
ordering the discord and chaos within,
preserving my life from utter destruction.
In the eye of the storm I hear the whisper of mercy,
the peace of those who are completely forgiven.

"I will instruct you and guide you,
I will teach you the way you should go.
I will counsel you with my ear to the Truth,
a keen and kindly eye fixed upon you.
Do not be like horse or mule, with no understanding,
whose course must be curbed with bridle and bit."

Many are the pangs of the wicked:
steadfast love surrounds those who trust God.
People of integrity, rejoice in God and be glad:
shout for joy all you that are true of heart.

Compassionate Friend, warm the frozen places of my fear, irrigate the deserts of my apathy, dismantle the wall around my pain and love, lift the burdens of my past, that I may be free to live in the joy of the Risen Christ.

THE GOD OF CREATION AND HISTORY

Refrain: *Praise to the Love that moves the stars*
and stirs the heart of the people.

LET those who serve you praise you, O God,
let the true of heart give you thanks.
Let the melodies of the strings be played,
accompanying our words in your praise.

For your Word, O God, is true,
your deeds reflect your covenant.
You love the justice of relationships made right,
the world is full of your steadfast love.

O God, you are the God of creation:
by your word was the universe made,
the numberless stars by the breath of your mouth.
You held the waters of the seas in the hollow of your hand,
you gathered to yourself all the treasures of the deep.

Let the whole earth be in awe of you,
all the inhabitants of the world greet you with joy.
For you spoke, and the wonderful deed was done;
you commanded, and it all came to pass.

O God, you are the God of history:
all the ways of the nations are but nothing in your sight.
You frustrate the devices of the peoples,
and your counsel and truth stand for ever,
the purpose of your heart to all generations.
Blessed are the people who put their trust in you,
whom you have chosen to serve a high destiny.

Not one of the children of earth can escape you;
all the inhabitants of the earth are in your sight.
You fashion all our hearts
and comprehend all our ways.

A ruler is not saved by a mighty army,
a warrior is not delivered by much strength.
A war horse is a vain hope for victory,
and by its great might it cannot save.

But your eye, O God, is on those who fear you,
who trust in your unfailing love.
You deliver them from the pangs of death,
and feed them in the time of famine.

We wait for you eagerly, O God,
for you are our hope and our shield.
Surely our hearts shall rejoice in you,
for we have trusted in your holy name.
Let your merciful kindness be upon us,
even as our hope is in you.

O Love, moving the sun and the moon and the stars, weave the pattern of glory to the bounds of the universe, even the cells of our being.

GOD THE BEARER OF PAIN

Refrain: *With the strings that are taut with pain*
compose new music of joy.

WE will bless you, O God, at all times,
your praise opening our lips.
We will exalt your name alone:
the afflicted will hear and be glad.
We give the Pain-bearer thanks:
we magnify the name of our God.

I sought your help and you answered,
you freed me from all my fears.
We look towards you and are radiant:
our faces shall not be ashamed.

The cry of the poor reaches your ears,
you saved us out of our trouble.
Your angel guards and protects us,
bringing your deliverance near.

So do we taste and see
how gracious and good is our God.
You meet us in the depth of our pain,
those who love you and fear you lack nothing.

Come, my children, listen to me:
I will teach you the way of our God.
Who among you relishes life,
wants time to enjoy good things?
Let no spite defile your tongue,
no lies fall from your lips.
Renounce the ways of evil,
pursue peace with all your heart.

Your eyes, O God, turn to the humble poor,
your ears to the cry of the needy and just.
You set your face against those who do wrong,
cutting off the memory of their deeds.

When those who do no harm cry for help,
you come close to their anguish and calm them.
Gently you embrace the broken in heart,
and revive the crushed in spirit.

Many are the afflictions of those who seek good,
but the pain-bearing God is with them.
You penetrate the heart of their suffering,
that they come to no lasting harm.

Evil rebounds on itself,
those consumed with hatred come to nothing.
O God, you redeem the life of your servants:
close to you, they will not be destroyed.

Pain-bearer God, in our affliction we sense your presence, moving with our
sufferings to redeem them, bringing joy out of tragedy, creating such music as the
world has not yet heard. We praise you with great praise.

THE QUIET IN THE LAND

Refrain: *Praise God who delivers the weak from the strong,*
               the needy from those who despoil them.

I AM angry at the proud and self-righteous,
yet I see their face in my own.
I wreak havoc in the lives of my neighbours,
seemingly concerned for the good of their souls.
By innuendo I slander a name,
prejudging the ones I dislike,
gossiping in pubs and in churches,
hypocritically enjoying the headlines.

Let us be put to shame and dishonour,
hawks that seek the destruction of life.
Let us be turned back and confounded,
who devise evil against our neighbours.
Let us be like chaff before the wind,
the angel of God driving us on.
Let our way be dark and slippery,
the hound of God pursuing us.
Let the nets of our devising ensnare us,
let us fall to ruin in them,
swallowed up in the pit we dug for others,
for the poor, the defenceless, the oppressed . . .

At such a turn in the world's affairs
the oppressed shall rejoice in the deliverance of God.
From the depth of their being they shall say,
Praise God who delivers the weak from the strong,
the needy from those who despoil them . . .

Malicious witnesses rise up,
spinning traps with their words,
making the innocent sign confessions
about things they know nothing of.
All that is good is called evil;
even if heard the truth is not known.

And yet I prayed for my enemies,
lost in bewildered confusion.
Crumpled with grief I prayed long
as if mourning a companion or brother.
My eyes looked to the ground
as if I were lamenting my mother.

But when I stumbled they laughed me to scorn
and gathered together against me.
As though I were a stranger I never knew
they slandered me without ceasing.
When I slipped they mocked me more and more,
and hissed at me through their teeth . . .

How long, O God, will you look from afar?
Rescue me from the grip of their teeth,
my life from the tearing of lions.
And I will give you thanks in the great congregation,
in the throng of the people I will praise you.

Let not the malicious triumph over their victims,
let not the mockers hate others with their eyes.
For they speak not words that make for peace,
but invent lies against those who are quiet in the
land.

They stretch their mouths to jeer,
they rub their hands with glee,
sweeping the poor off their parcel of land,
claiming – As far as you can see, all is mine . . .

And you also have seen, O God:
do not be silent and hidden away.
Stir yourself, be awake for justice,
for the cause of the poor and oppressed.
Judge us in your righteousness,
let not the proud triumph,
let them not say, "Good, we have our heart's desire;"
let them not say, "Good, we have destroyed them."

Refrain: *Praise God who delivers the weak from the strong,*
                    the needy from those who despoil them.

Let those who rejoice at others' hurt
be completely disgraced and confounded.
Let them be clothed with shame and dishonour
who trample the face of the needy,
exalting themselves at the expense of the poor.
But let those who long for justice
shout for joy and be glad:
let them say, "Great is God!
You delight in all those who serve you."
Then my tongue shall speak of your righteous ways,
and of your praise all the day long.

*Disarm the mighty, O God, and calm their fears. Let scales fall from their eyes,
let them weep tears of repentance, that they may see their enemies as human beings,
and come to know them as the only friends who bear the gift of their salvation,
in Jesus, powerless and victorious in love for us.*

THE JUDGE WHO DOES RIGHT

Refrain: *Pierce to the heart of our wickedness,*
            abandon us not to our doom.

TRANSGRESSION whispers to the wicked, deep in their hearts:
there is no fear of God in their eyes.
They flatter themselves with their own reflection,
imagining their wickedness is a secret for ever.

The words of their mouths are mischief and deceit:
they have ceased to act wisely and never do good.
Lying awake in the night, plotting with malice,
they set themselves on a path that is crooked,
no longer aware of the evil they do.

Your steadfast love, O God, extends through the universe,
your faithfulness to the furthest stars.
Your justice is like the high mountains,
your judgment as the great deep.

So the Judge of all the earth will do right.
You will save us, frail children of the dust:
precious indeed is your kindness and love.
The children of earth find refuge in your shade,
you entertain them to a feast in your house.
You give them water to drink from the river of delight:
for with you is the well of life,
and in your light do we see light.

Continue your goodness to those who know you,
your saving ways to the true of heart.
Let not the foot of the proud trample us,
nor the hand of the arrogant push us aside.
Under the weight of their scheming may they crumple,
their will to do evil extinguished for ever.

O God, wise and discerning in all that you do, deliver us from the illusion that we are better than others; rather than condemning one another, may we come together and kneel in humility, knowing only your mercy and truth, in Jesus Christ our Saviour.

DOGGED TRUST IN GOD

Refrain: *In meeting the powers of evil*
let us deepen our trust in God.

Do not fret yourself because of the ungodly,
do not be envious of those who do evil.
For then you become as one of them,
putting yourself in the wrong.
They will soon fade away like grass,
withering like the leaves in drought.
Simply trust in God, and do good:
we shall dwell in the land and graze safely.

Let us delight in your company, O God,
and you will give us our heart's desire.
Let us commit our lives to your goodness,
let us cast all our cares on your shoulders.
Let us trust you to act with justice,
to deliver us in your own good time.
You will make our vindication shine clear as the light,
our integrity bright as the noonday sun.

Let us be still and wait for you patiently,
bearing the tension that all is not well,
calming the restless desire to be certain,
in advance of the day of your coming.
Let us not be vexed when others prosper,
when they weave their evil designs.
May we let go of anger and rage,
refusing to let envy move us to evil.

For the wicked shall be cut down:
those who wait for God shall inherit the land.
In a while the ungodly shall be no more:
we shall look for them in their place:
we shall find it deserted, left to the wind.
The humiliated shall inherit the earth,
they shall enjoy the abundance of peace.

Refrain: *In meeting the powers of evil*
               let us deepen our trust in God.

The ungodly plot against the righteous
and gnash at them with their teeth.
But you, O God, will laugh them to scorn,
for you know their overthrow comes soon.

The ungodly have drawn the sword from the sheath,
they have aimed their arrows at the poor and the needy,
slaughtering those who walk in truth.
Their swords shall pierce their own hearts,
their arrows and bows shall be broken.
Sin turns in on itself,
and destroys the works of the wicked.

Though the righteous have but a little,
it is better than the hoards of the wicked.
The strong arm of the ungodly shall be broken:
God upholds those who are true of heart.

God cares for the lives of the humble poor,
and their heritage shall be theirs for ever.
They shall not be put to shame in evil days,
but in time of famine they shall eat their fill.
As for the ungodly they shall perish,
they are the enemies of God:
like fuel in a furnace they will be consumed,
like smoke they will vanish away.

The ungodly borrow but never repay:
but the poor are often generous and give.
Those who are blessed by God will inherit the land,
those whom God has cursed will be cut down.
If our steps are guided by God,
and if we delight in God's way,
though we stumble we shall not fall headlong,
for you, O God, will steady us with your hand.

I have been young and now I am old,
but I never saw the good man forsaken,
or his children begging their bread.
The righteous are gracious and lend,
and their children shall be blessed in the land.
Turn from evil and do good,
and you will dwell in the land for ever.
For you, O God, love what is just,
you will not forsake those who are faithful.
But the ways of the unjust will perish for ever,
the seed of the ungodly will be destroyed.

The righteous will inherit the land,
and they will dwell in it for ever.
The mouths of the just utter wisdom,
and their tongues speak what is right.
The law of God is in their hearts,
and their footsteps will not slip.
The ungodly watch out for the righteous,
and seek occasion to slay them.
But God will not abandon them to their power,
nor let them be condemned when they are judged.

We wait for you, O God, and we hold to your Way,
and you will raise us up to inherit the land,
to see the ungodly when they wither away.
I have seen the wicked in terrifying power,
spreading themselves like luxuriant trees.
I passed by again and they were gone,
I searched for them but they could not be found.

Observe the blameless and consider the upright,
for people of peace will have prosperity.
Deliverance for the righteous will come:
O God, you will save them in the time of trouble.

Refrain: *In meeting the powers of evil*
            let us deepen our trust in God.

Enable us in these our days,
we who are the privileged few,
help us to lend our strength to the weak,
our voices to the small and the voiceless.
Help us to sound our compassion and anger,
to strive with those who oppress the downtrodden,
showing them their greed and malice and fear,
helping them to face their enemy within,
that they may open their hearts to be generous.
May they do the same for those they exploit,
that their wickedness too may vanish away.
Together redeem us, long-suffering God,
bring us all to share in your peace.

*Be with us, O God, as we struggle for a more just world, yet remind us that our
actions so often tighten the mesh that binds the oppressed. Keep us from pride in
our own strength, and keep us from despair when evil seems entrenched. Renew
our trust in your good purposes for us all. Give us the gift of discernment, that
we may know when to strive in the power of your Spirit, and when to be still and
wait for your deliverance. Come in your good time, but come soon!*

A CRY FROM THE MIDST OF PAIN AND GUILT

Refrain: From the power of guilt and pain
                save me and heal me, O Christ.

O GOD, do you rebuke me in your anger?
Do you chasten me in fierce displeasure?
Is it your arrows that pierce me,
your hand come heavy upon me?
With no health in my flesh, do you punish me,
in sternness of love, for my sins?

The tide of my wrongs sweeps over my head,
their weight is a burden too heavy to bear.
My wounds stink and fester through folly,
I am bowed down with grieving all the day long.
My loins are filled with a burning pain,
there is no sound part in my flesh.
I am numbed and stricken to the ground,
I groan in the anguish of my heart.

The pounding of my heart comes to your ears,
my desire for love, my stumbling on the road.
My deep sighing is not hidden from you,
my longing for kindness and the touch that heals.

My heart is in tumult, my strength fails me,
even the light of my eyes has gone from me.
My companions draw back from my affliction,
my kinsfolk stare afar at my sores.

I am like the deaf and hear nothing,
like those whose mouths are sealed.
I have become as one who cannot hear,
in whose mouth there is no retort.

I falter on the edge of the abyss,
my pain is with me continually.
I confess my wickedness with tears,
I shudder with sorrow for my sin.

Refrain: *From the power of guilt and pain*
                save me and heal me, O Christ.

Those who seek my life lay their snares,
those who desire my hurt spread evil tales,
murmuring slanders all the day long.
I prayed, Let them never exult over me,
those who laugh harshly when I stumble and fall.

My enemies without cause are strong,
those who hate me wrongfully are many.
Those who repay evil for good are against me,
they blame me for what I did right.

But in you, O God, I have put my trust,
and you will answer me in saving judgment.
Do not forsake me, do not go far from me;
hasten to my help, O God of my salvation.

For I know you enter the heart of our anguish,
you take to yourself the pain of the universe,
you bear the marks of our sins,
you endure and still you forgive.

It is not for our sin that we suffer,
nor for the wrongs of our forebears.
It is that your name may be glorified,
that in us your purpose be known.
Your vulnerable love works without ceasing
to draw us from despair into glory.

*Saviour and Healer, present in the midst of our distress, forgiving our sin and
relieving our suffering, enable us to deepen our trust in your Spirit at work within
us, that your Love may overwhelm us with joy and your Hand guide us in the
dance of freedom.*

ANGER HUMAN AND DIVINE

Refrain: *Mysterious is the God who throws us to the ground*
and continually raises us up.

I WILL keep watch over my words,
so that I do not offend with my tongue.
I will put a muzzle on my mouth,
while the wicked are in my presence.

How can I keep silent in our day,
as I see the hypocrisies around me,
the poor defrauded of land,
the dwelling place of God dishonoured?

Now that my eyes have been opened,
it is impossible not to be angry.
I cannot be aware and stay calm:
it goes against the grain of my being.

I tried to hold my tongue and say nothing,
refusing to be rash, keeping silent.
But the pain grew intolerable,
my heart burned hot within me.
While I mused the fire burst into flame,
and I spoke from the depth of my being.

Possessed by the demon of anger,
swept along by the vortex of rage,
I was an easy target for the powerful,
a well-aimed blow and I fell.

Yet I need the fire in my belly,
its heat and its light to move me.
I need it to spur me to action,
rage become love in the service of others.

Refrain: *Mysterious is the God who throws us to the ground
              and continually raises us up.*

Yet I know how fleeting is my life:
O God, let me remember my end,
and the number of my days.
You have made my years but a handsbreath,
my whole span is as nothing before you.

Thinking we stand secure,
we are but a breath of wind,
our lives but a passing shadow.
The riches we heap are like autumn leaves,
golden and brittle to those who gather them.

And now, O God, what is my hope?
Truly my hope is in you.
Deliver me from the trap of my sins,
do not make me the butt of fools.

I was dumb, I did not open my mouth,
silenced now by the thought of my sin.
Your arm is straightening my crookedness,
a pain not easy to bear.

With rebukes you humble me low,
you cause my fair looks to decay,
like a moth you destroy my possessions.
Surely we are but a breath,
as nothing in the sight of your eyes.

Hear my prayer and give ear to my cry:
do not be silent at my tears.
I am but a stranger with you,
a passing guest as my ancestors were.

Turn your anger away from me,
that I may breathe awhile and be glad,
before I go hence
and am no more seen.

So I rely on your kindness alone,
entrusting myself to your mercy,
even to the gates of my death,
down to the depths of the grave.

O God of mysterious anger, may we not imagine you destructive as we are in our rage, but recognize your piercing heat and light serving the truth, your fiercely loving anger overcoming our murdering and mortality, in Jesus Christ our Saviour.

FAITH REJOICING AND FAITH STRUGGLING

Refrain: *In the strivings and rejoicings of faith*
              may our search and our trust give you praise.

I WAITED patiently for you, my God,
and at last you heard my cry.
You lifted me out of the icy torrent,
you drew me out of the quicksand and mire.
You set my feet on solid ground,
making firm my foothold on rock.
No longer am I empty and lost:
you have given my life new meaning.

You have put a new song in my mouth,
a song of thanksgiving and praise.
Many will recognize your wondrous deeds:
they will be glad and put their trust in you.
Blessed are those who have made you their hope,
who have not turned to pride and to lying,
nor to wandering in pursuit of false gods.

Great are the wonderful things you have done,
marvellous are your thoughts and desires.
There is none to be compared with you:
were I to declare everything you have done,
your deeds are more than I am able to express.

We cannot buy your favour with bribes,
you were not pleased with the sacrifices of old.
It is the gift of my heart and my will
that you seek in your long-suffering love.
You have softened the wax in my ears,
I hear you at last and respond:
open and attentive I listen to your voice.

Dear God, I long to do your will.
Your law of love delights my heart.
I have not hidden your salvation in silence,
I have told of your resurrection and glory.
I have not kept back the glad news of deliverance,
your faithfulness, justice, and truth.

So may your truth ever protect me,
your steadfast mercy and love ever be close –
yes, even when troubles overwhelm me,
more numerous than the hairs of my head,
when my sins overtake me and I cannot hear,
and my heart fails within me.

Let those who seek my life to take it away,
let them be put to shame and utterly confounded.
Let those who gloat with the laughter of scorn,
let them be turned back and disgraced.

So may I turn and be glad in you,
so that those who love your salvation may say,
Great and wonderful is God.
In my poverty and need and oppression,
yet you are with me, caring for me.
Yes, I am assured of my faith,
and yes, I still strive to believe.
You are my helper and deliverer:
make no long delay, my Saviour, my God.

*O God of truth and mercy, whose voice we miss amidst the distractions and noise
of our lives, penetrate to the core of our being, that we may hear and be glad,
knowing ourselves accepted in your love, able once again to live in your truth and
forgiveness; through Jesus Christ our Saviour.*

WHO CONDEMNS?

Refrain: *With judgment and mercy, O God,*
               redeem us in the light of your eyes.

BLESSED are those who care for the poor and the helpless,
who are kind to the outcast within them.
God will deliver them in the day of their trouble,
rescuing the child who is battered and torn.
God will guard them and preserve their life:
they shall be counted as blessed in the land.

O God, you will not give us over to the will of our enemies,
to hatred within and to blame without.
In the day of our calamity you will sustain us,
as warring turbulence threatens our life.

Dear God, be merciful towards me,
heal me for I have sinned against you.
My enemies, within and without, speak evil of me:
''When will you die and your name perish for ever?''

They mouth empty words when they see me,
and mischief stirs in their hearts.
They talk among themselves in the street,
whispering suspicion against me.

They smile at the revealing of my sins,
gloating in triumph at my downfall,
cackling like demons that claw at me,
plucking me down to the mire.

''You are wracked with a deadly disease,
you will not rise again from where you lie.''
Even my bosom friend whom I trusted,
who shared my bread, looks down on me.

O God, come down and raise me up,
struggling from the pit in anger and truth,
wrestling with my enemies in my love for them,
dependent together on mercy.
So shall we know that you delight in us,
setting us before your face for ever.

Cleanse my whole being that I may see truly,
that revenge may not brood in my heart.
Keep me from believing all strangers are hostile,
let me see with the eyes of compassion.

May I think good of those who strive against me,
however full of malice seem their hearts.
Heap burning coals of love on our heads:
melt our fears with the flame of your desire.

Burn out from us all that breeds evil,
that we may no longer hurt or destroy.
May we follow the way of justice,
and be redeemed to your glory and joy.

Blessed be God,
the God of all peoples,
at all times and all places,
now and for ever.

Merciful God, prone as we are to blame others and to hate ourselves, take from our eyes the dust that blinds us, that we may treat one another by the light of your compassion, and in the Spirit of Jesus Christ who is the Light of the world.

YEARNING FOR GOD

Refrain: *Why are you so full of heaviness, O my soul,*
and why so rebellious within me?
Put your trust in God,
patiently wait for the dawn,
and you will then praise
your deliverer and your God.

As a deer longs for streams of water,
so longs my soul for you, O God.
My soul is thirsty for the living God:
when shall I draw near to see your face?
My tears have been my food in the night:
all day long they ask me, Where now is your God?
As I pour out my soul in distress,
I remember how I went to the temple of God,
with shouts and songs of thanksgiving,
a multitude keeping high festival.

My soul is heavy within me: therefore I remember you
from the land of Jordan and from the hills of Hermon.
Deep calls to deep in the roar of the waterfalls,
all your waves and your torrents have gone over me.
Surely, O God, you will show me mercy in the daytime,
and at night I will sing your praise, O God my God.
I will say to God, my rock, Why have you forgotten me?
Why must I go like a mourner because the enemy oppresses me?
Like a sword piercing my bones, my enemies have mocked me,
asking me all day long, Where now is your God?

O God, take up my cause and strive for me
with a godless people that knows no mercy.
Save me from the grip of cunning and lies,
for you are my God and my strength.
Why must you cast me away from your presence?
Why must I be clothed in rags, humiliated by my enemy?
O send out your light and your truth and let them lead me,
let them guide me to your holy hill and to your dwelling.
Then I shall go to the altar of God, the God of my joy and
    delight,
and to the harp I shall sing your praises, O God my God.

Loving God, as we join our cries with those who are deeply depressed and in despair, renew in us the spirit of hope, the yearning for life in you alone, and the expectancy that even when every door is closed, yet you will surprise us with joy.

CAST OFF BY GOD?

Refrain: *Is the wood of the cross now in splinters?*
                  Does the tree of salvation still stand?

WE have heard with our ears, O God,
our ancestors have told us,
what things you did in their days,
how you drove out the tribes before us
and caused us to root and to grow.
For it was not by their swords
that they possessed the land,
nor did their own power get them the victory,
but your right hand, your holy arm,
and the light of your countenance upon them.
It was out of sheer love that you did this,
out of your care and delight.

You reign over us their descendants:
by your power do we strike our enemies:
in your name alone do we tread them down.
We do not trust in long bow and sword,
but only in you to deliver us,
putting our adversaries to confusion.
In you alone is our boast,
giving thanks to your name without ceasing.

But now you have cast us off and brought us to shame,
you do not go out with our armies.
You have given us as sheep to be butchered,
and our foes plunder us at will.
You have scattered us among the nations,
and made a profitless sale.
You have made us the scorn of our neighbours,
mocked and derided by those around us.

You have made us a byword among the peoples:
they dismiss us with eyes full of hatred.
Our disgrace is before us all the day long,
and shame has covered our face,
at the voice of the slanderer and reviler,
at the sight of the enemy and avenger.

All this calamity has fallen upon us,
even though we have not forgotten you.
We have not betrayed your covenant,
our hearts have not turned back,
nor have our steps strayed from your paths.

Yet you have crushed us in the haunts of jackals,
and covered us with the deepest darkness.
If we had forgotten your name,
or stretched out our hands to strange gods,
would you not have searched it out,
knowing as you do the secrets of our hearts?
But for your sake we are killed all the day long,
we are counted as sheep for the slaughter.

Rouse yourself, O God, why do you sleep?
Awake, do not cast us off for ever.
Why do you hide your face
and forget our misery and oppression?
Our souls are bowed to the dust,
our bellies cleave to the ground.
Arise, O God, and help us,
and redeem us for your mercy's sake.

Strange how all this should surprise us –
the evil we thought was elsewhere
runs through the heart of each one of us.
No wonder we sense your eclipse, O God,
boasting you are always behind us.

Refrain: *Is the wood of the cross now in splinters?*
                Does the tree of salvation still stand?

Renew in us your covenant with Earth,
that we may respect one another,
even those who hate and despise us.
However oppressed we may be,
and must strive to disarm the oppressor,
keep hope of your forgiveness alive,
transform our thirst for revenge,
bring us home with weeping and joy.

And yet we are being too kind,
too easy and bland in the face of great evil?
What of the cry of the Holocaust,
of the sheep slaughtered by jackals?
What of the voice of those without name,
a number, a badge, for aliens despised?
Naked they went to the chambers of gas,
hair, clothes and rings left behind.
Their corpses were piled into ovens,
their ashes scattered on lakes that were bitter.

What of those who drove the trains,
who herded like cattle folk like ourselves,
who patrolled the barbed wire of the camps,
who delivered by lorry the canisters of gas?
What of those who locked the doors,
who put out the lights, melted the gold,
who turned their skin into lampshades?

O God, why are you silent?
O God, answer those who accuse you.
Why have you forgotten the wretched of the earth?
What profit do you gain from this their affliction?

*O God of Love – if indeed you are Love, for the howls of suffering have hidden
your face – show us again in the Crucified One the eyes telling us that you are
there, at the heart of the desolate cries.*

A ROYAL CELEBRATION

Refrain: *Clothe us with the splendour and glory
that shines through justice and mercy.*

My heart is aflame with fine phrases,
I make my song for the great king:
my tongue is the pen of a skilled writer.
You are the fairest of the children of earth:
grace flows from your lips,
for God has blessed you for ever and ever.

Take the sword to protect the weak,
defeating those who would threaten them.
Ride on in the cause of truth,
and for the sake of justice and mercy.
Your enemies will do well to tremble,
your arrows will be sharp in their hearts.

Your divine throne endures for ever,
the sceptre of your realm is a sceptre of equity.
You love righteousness and hate evil:
so God has anointed you with the oil of gladness,
choosing you to serve for the sake of the people.

Your garments are fragrant with myrrh, aloes, and cassia:
music from ivory palaces makes your heart glad.
Daughters of kings are among your noble women:
the queen is at your side in gold of Ophir.

Hear, O daughter, consider and incline your ear:
forget your own people and your father's house.
The king desires your beauty:
he is your lord: bow down before him.
The richest among the people, O daughter of Tyre,
shall entreat your favour with gifts.

Refrain: *Clothe us with the splendour and glory*
               that shines through justice and mercy.

The princess in her chamber is being robed
with garments of cloth of gold.
In robes of brilliant colours
she is led to your presence, O king.
Her bridesmaids follow in procession,
with joy and gladness they form her train:
they enter the palace with songs of delight.

So the generations pass,
as children grow strong and their elders fade.
May the old become wise and the young bring us hope.
And I will make God's name known,
whose reign has no end.
All the peoples will praise you, O God,
throughout the generations.

We praise you, O God,
for the gift of yourself in the Infant King:
Jesus, sovereign ruler of all,
in whom is our royal destiny too:
celebrants at the banquet of heaven,
guests at the great marriage feast,
gloriously singing in triumphal procession,
our ancestors and descendants with us,
joyful in the communion of saints.

Dear God, we offer you our lives this day,
the gift of love in our hearts and our loins,
the incense of prayer, the myrrh of our suffering,
the gold of all that we hold most dear,
that you may create through our loyal obedience,
such wonders as pass our imagining.

*Lift up our hearts, O glorious God, and renew in us the hope of a marvellous
destiny, a life of incomparable splendour, crowned with the love and peace that
pass understanding, in Jesus Christ, our Servant-King.*

THE GOD OF POWERS

Refrain: *You are for us the God of the powers,*
                 a safe stronghold, the God of all peoples.

GOD is our refuge and strength,
a very present help in time of trouble.
Therefore we shall not be afraid,
even though the earth be moved,
even though the mountains should crumble
and fall into the sea,
even though the waters should foam and rage,
assault the cliffs and make them shudder.

There is a river whose streams make glad the city of God.
Here is God's dwelling place and it will stand firm.
God's rescue dawns like the morning light,
God's voice echoes through every land.
When powerful nations panic and totter
and the whole world comes crashing down,

Come and see, stand in awe
at the powerful things God will do on the earth,
putting an end to all war in the world,
breaking the bow, shattering the spear into splinters,
throwing our weapons on the fire.
"Be still and know that I am God:
exalted among the nations,
my name known at last on the earth."

At the still centre of the turning world, may we simply rest and be, trusting again
the promise that all shall be made new in the bringing of the powers of this world
to serve the purposes of God's greater Peace.

THE WORSHIP OF THE PEOPLE OF GOD

Refrain: *As citizens of one world*
your people give you praise.

CLAP your hands, all you peoples:
cry aloud to God with shouts of joy.
Approach the presence of God with awe,
the great sovereign over all the earth.

O God, you have called us to serve the peoples,
that they may come to acknowledge your glory.
You have made us stewards of your gifts,
that we may not boast and be proud.
You have loved us and blessed us with a goodly heritage,
overflowing with all that we need.

Let us join the procession in praise of your name,
with trumpets and horns and the sound of rejoicing.
We sing praises, sing praises to you, O God,
we sing praises, sing praises to your name.

For you are sovereign over all the earth:
let us praise your name with well-wrought psalm.
You are the ruler of all the peoples,
wise and just in your dealings.

Those who give counsel gather together
as the people of the God of Abraham.
For even the mighty ones of the earth
are become the servants of God,
the God who is greatly to be praised.

Living, loving God, draw the peoples of faith closer together, ancient and ever-new, that we may worship you today in spirit and in truth.

THE CITY OF GOD

Refrain: *May the cities and lands of this world*
             be transformed by the Spirit of God.

O GOD, you are greatly to be praised
in the city of your dwelling place.
High and beautiful is the holy mountain:
it is the joy of the whole earth.

Here on Mount Zion stands the city
where you reign with just and steady hand.
Your rule is firm and secure,
strong as the walls and ramparts.

Strangers who approach are amazed,
the powerful of the earth dumbfounded.
Trembling takes hold of the proud,
anguish seizes the hostile,
like the howl of the harsh east wind
that splinters the ships on the rocks.

We call your mercies to mind,
here in the midst of your temple.
You govern the peoples with justice,
even to the ends of the earth.

Pilgrim, walk round the city,
count all her towers,
examine her walls with care,
consider well her strongholds.

So may we tell those who come after,
that here they may rest secure,
for our God reigns for ever and ever,
who will guide us to all eternity.

Refrain: *May the cities and lands of this world*
              be transformed by the Spirit of God.

Such was the place of your worship and dwelling,
sacred, O God, to your people of old.
Now may you dwell in each of our hearts,
may every city be the place of your dwelling.

So may we worship you in spirit and truth,
may recognize you in streets and in squares,
in a common life of justice and peace,
in compassion and freedom under the law.

Bring the light, O God, that will one day shine
brighter than the sun and the moon and the stars,
the light of the Christ to illumine the dark,
the face that transfigures the city to glory.

Gracious God, you have called us to the freedom of your City. So shape our lives in the ways of justice that we may become worthy of that citizenship that you have bestowed upon us, in the communion of your saints and in the fellowship of Jesus Christ.

THE HOLLOWNESS OF WEALTH

Refrain: *Where your treasure is,*
                there will your heart be also.

HEAR this, all you peoples;
listen, inhabitants of the world,
all children of the earth,
both rich and poor together.
My mouth shall speak wisdom,
the thoughts of my heart be full of understanding.
I will reveal the secret of a riddle,
unfolding a mystery to the sound of the lyre.

Why should I be afraid in times of trouble,
when the cruel and the greedy triumph,
those who put their trust in great wealth,
and boast of the abundance of their riches?

No one may ransom a sister or brother,
no one give God a price for them,
so that they may live for ever
and never see the grave:
to ransom their lives is so costly
we must abandon the idea for ever.

For we see the prosperous die,
and perish with the foolish and ignorant,
leaving their wealth to others.
The tomb is their home for ever,
their dwelling through all generations,
despite their estates named after them.
The wealthy in all their pomp –
they are just like the beasts – they perish.

Refrain: *Where your treasure is,*
              there will your heart be also.

This is the lot of the arrogant,
who are pleased with their words
and trust in themselves.
They are destined to die like sheep:
death is their shepherd,
they cannot avoid their end.
Their good looks will fade in the tomb,
and their grandeur will follow them.

But God will ransom my life,
God will snatch me from the power of the grave.
I will not be afraid when neighbours grow rich,
when the wealth of their households increases.
For they will take nothing away when they die,
nor will their wealth go down to them.

Though they thought highly of themselves while they lived,
and were praised for their worldly success,
they will go to the company of their ancestors,
who will never again see the sun.
The wealthy in all their pomp –
they are just like the beasts – they perish.

Living God, may our contemplation of death free us from envy and greed, that
we may be content to travel light in this world, undistracted by the babel of
possessions and in the Spirit of the One who had nowhere to lay his head, Jesus
Christ our Saviour.

THE JUDGMENT OF GOD

Refrain: *Your eyes are fierce with love,*
                your hands are gentle in judgment.

FROM the midst of the glory of the sun,
from the mountain top of your appearing,
you come to us in perfect beauty,
the judge of the earth doing all things well.

You come to us, you do not keep silent,
you sear us with the flames of your truth,
you devour the chaff of our sins:
awesome is this face of your love.

We have failed to worship you in truth,
we have been disloyal to your covenant,
content with repeating mere words,
self-important in the display of our ceremonies.

We have not obeyed your will,
colluding with those who thieve and betray,
loosening our tongues in slander and gossip,
even lying against kith and kin.

Open our eyes and ears, O God,
we who have been so blind and deaf,
seduced by the glamour and dazzle around us,
lulled by the weavers of magic with words.

No better are we than your people of old,
seeking to please you with smoking burnt sacrifice,
thinking you relished animals' flesh,
that this was the worship you sought.

But all the beasts of the forest are yours,
and so are the cattle on a thousand hills;
you know all the birds of the air,
the grasshoppers of the field are in your sight.

Refrain: *Your eyes are fierce with love,*
              your hands are gentle in judgment.

You own the very gifts that we bring you,
all things come to us from out of your hand.
You give them to us to enjoy
and to share with others in need.

Sacrificial love is the altar of worship
where you touch the lives of the needy,
humbled as we are by all that you give us,
judged by those more generous than we.

Renew in us the covenant of old,
may we be faithful to the promises we made,
the vows over gifts to be holy with you,
in deed and in truth to follow your way.

You thunder so fiercely in love for us,
you whisper so gently in judgment,
lowering the walls of defence
that surround our self-centred complaints.

So often we live for ourselves,
indifferent to the needs of the oppressed,
passing by the homeless under the arches,
refusing to hear how you judge us through them.

Turn us around, compassionate judge,
show us the face of your pain:
it is we who add to your burden,
as you endure the cost of redeeming.

In the day of our need we cry out to you,
offering our sorrowing hearts,
trusting that you will forgive us,
and refine us in the flame of your love.

*Come, living Christ, with burning coals and purge our lips; come with the
judgment that saves and gives us back our sense of worth because it matters what
we do; come with passionate desire and sweep us into your arms; come with the
love that will not let us go.*